Mythologems

Marie-Louise von Franz, Honorary Patron

**Studies in Jungian Psychology
by Jungian Analysts**

Daryl Sharp, General Editor

MYTHOLOGEMS

Incarnations of
the Invisible World

JAMES HOLLIS

To Jill, to our children, Taryn and Timothy, Jonah and Seah,
and to the people of the C.G. Jung Educational Center of Houston.
I also thank Daryl Sharp and Inner City Books for sharing the
gift of analytical psychology with so many others.

See final pages for more titles in this series by James Hollis and others

National Library of Canada Cataloguing in Publication Data

Hollis, James, 1940-
   Mythologems: incarnations of the invisible world
   / James Hollis.

(Studies in Jungian psychology by Jungian analysts; 109)
Includes bibliographical references and index.

ISBN 1-894574-10-9

1. Myth—Psychological aspects.
2. Jungian psychology.
I. Title. II. Series.

BL313.H64 2004   291.1'3'019   C2003-907210-X

INNER CITY BOOKS
Box 1271, Station Q, Toronto, ON M4T 2P4, Canada

Telephone (416) 927-0355 / FAX (416) 924-1814
Web site: www.innercitybooks.net / E-mail: admin@innercitybooks.net

Honorary Patron: Marie-Louise von Franz.
Publisher and General Editor: Daryl Sharp.
Senior Editor: Victoria Cowan.

INNER CITY BOOKS was founded in 1980 to promote the
understanding and practical application of the work of C.G. Jung.

Cover: "Herstory," relief print by Vicki Cowan; 14" x 4".

Printed and bound in Canada by University of Toronto Press Incorporated

CONTENTS

What seest thou else
In the dark backward and abysm of time?
—Shakespeare, *The Tempest.*

The deep is the unsayable.
—Ludwig Wittgenstein, *Philosophical Investigations.*

The lord whose oracle is in Delphi neither speaks nor
conceals but gives a sign.
—Heraclitus, *Fragments.*

The world is full of signs, and the wise will begin to see them.
—Plotinus, *Enneads.*

Signatures of all things I am here to read, seaspawn and
seawrack, the nearing tide.
—James Joyce, *Ulysses.*

Whereof one cannot speak, thereof one must remain silent.
—Ludwig Wittgenstein, *Philosophical Investigations.*

Introduction
Through a Glass Darkly

The word "myth" originates, as virtually all words do, in a metaphor. Our words begin, somewhere, way back when, as radical perceptions, as amazements born of experience, and later become image incarnated in speech. So, interestingly enough, the etymology of myth comes from the metaphor "to squint."

Squinting suggests that one sees something only dimly, only partially, only narrowly, but also intimates that something still remains unseen. Squinting—beloved by visual artists—also simplifies, reveals the essence. The word "myopia" suggests a squinty eye, a lack of clarity. We also have the word "mystery," to suggest how much lies beyond our ken. "Mum's the word," an oxymoron, suggests the acknowledged mystery which must not be spoken.

All of our kenning *(koernen, kann,* can) sees only a short way into all that largeness. So myth carries from its origin, shrouded in mystery, and through a glass dimly, the intimation, respect, awe, frustration and longing for something larger, much larger. That *numinosity* (from the metaphor "to nod," as something which bows toward us, acknowledges us, summons us) is our source, our home away from home, and our journey's end.

A "mythologem" is a single, fundamental element, or motif, of any myth. The motifs of ascent or descent are mythologems. The hero's quest embodies two such mythologems: the hero and the quest, each of which has a discernible lineage and separable meaning, and yet synergistically enlarge each other.

This is my second book on myth,[1] so either there is a need

---

[1] The first was *Tracking the Gods: the Place of Myth in Modern Life.*

out there that beckons to me, or I am alone in my fascination. In any case, I keep returning to the idea of myth and am compelled to reflect upon it over and over.

To my mind, myth is perhaps the most important psychological and cultural construct of our time. It is not only that the concept of myth has degenerated in popular parlance into something synonymous with falsehood. Or that myth, as it has been said, is someone else's religion. It is that, in a culture committed to the world of matter, access to the invisible world—which myth makes possible, along with its two chief instruments, metaphor and symbol—has never been more critical in allowing some balance of the spirit.

Clearly, we live in a culture of great spiritual impoverishment: addictive materialism makes us slaves to surfaces; fundamentalist clamor makes us fearful and anxious; and distracting, banal ideologies diminish rather than enlarge the journey of the soul.

We cannot, by definition, know the infinite, possess the gods, divine the invisible, but we are nonetheless the playthings of their power. We are invested with this energy at birth, experience its autonomy on a daily basis, develop inexorably toward personal annihilation, and yet universally yearn for meaning and connection.

Such energy is invisible, though transiently tangible when it invests in image. We can only render it conscious when it has incarnated. Such images are found in our body, in our emotional storms, in the track of our histories, in dreams which disturb sleep, and in our desires and aspirations. We hunger for meaning, for God, for love, for connection. Simultaneously we hurtle toward extinction in seeking sleep, death, the arms of the beloved—all through the great darkness in which we walk.

This energy which, as Dante put it, moves the sun and all the stars, which invests the newborn, and transforms itself through multiple lives and deaths, then dematerializes back into itself, is perceptible only in image. Tracking the image, then, is tracking the gods. "The gods" here are the personified metaphors of such energies. To call them gods is not to reify them in service to ego's need, except in the mind of the fundamentalist; rather it is to accord them respect for what they are, the dynamic energies of the cosmos and the psychodynamics of the individual.

By avoiding metaphysics we make epistemology possible. That is, by refusing to concretize the infinite in the trappings of finitude, we make it possible to approach the unknowable. We are "winking" when we use the term "the gods," as a sign of our respect for the autonomy of such energies, and our conscious use of a fiction (from *facere,* to make). Since we employ fictions all the time in our varied discourses, not to recognize them consciously as fictions is to be bewitched into literalism.

Why use the word "gods" rather than simply "energies"? The reason is that there is still enough potency in that word to evoke respect, and respect is our way of honoring those energies. I mean no slight to monotheists of whatever persuasion, but ask them to recall that it is an act of impiety not to remember that all images of divinity are metaphors, lest they no longer be divinities but artifacts of ego consciousness, better known as idols. Further, it is important to recall that, metaphorically, there is not one god but many, which is to say, many manifestations of this opaque yet ever-renewing source from whence we spring.

Our use of the expression "the gods" is thus a conscious, heuristic choice leading to deepened encounter, remaining open-ended, respectful and useful. As Owen Barfield once observed,

> There may be times when what is most needed is, not so much a new discovery or a new idea as a different "slant"; I mean a comparatively slight readjustment in our way of looking at the things and ideas on which attention is already fixed.[2]

---

[2] *Saving the Appearances: A Study in Idolatry,* p. 11.

I use the word "myth" in this book in three ways: 1) as psychodynamic image, 2) as personal scenario, or 3) as tribal value system.

Myth as psychodynamic image

An image is a structure capable of carrying energy and, when so charged, has the power to evoke energic response within us. Like to like, or dissimilar to dissimilar, the evocation of something in us moves us whether we will it or not. Our ancestors were right to personify love and rage as gods, for they are powerful possessions of the spirit by affectively charged experiences. Whoever has been transported to the heights of ecstasy and plunged to the depths of despair has known the god who has already known him. Whoever embodies rage has been possessed by Ares, the god whose crimson energy may just as quickly depart after it has been expressed through the person. When blood lust possesses a nation, or when Homer describes Achilles' eyes as "furnace doors ajar" after the death of his friend Patroclus,[3] the god is at its visible work.

Myth as personal scenario

While any of us in any moment may be seized by a particular mythologem, we may also come to recognize that we are often bound to life-long scenarios which silently but constantly reveal themselves through the conduct of our lives. For example, due to deeply-rooted unconscious assumptions received from our family of origin, we may forever seek assurances that we are seen, heard, valued. Or we may devote our lives to the healing of others, having learned early on that a fragile parent could only be available through subservience of the child's needs to the needs of the wounded parent. The list of such examples is infinite. The chief work of analysis, or the reward of maturity, is to discern

---

[3] Homer, *War Music*, p. 63.

such scenarios, or personal myths, at work in one's life. Only then are new choices possible.

In *The Middle Passage* I noted how the collision of such myths with our natural path of individuation reaches the surface as symptomatology. In *Creating a Life* and *On This Journey We Call Our Life* I suggested some ways in which one might go about identifying one's personal myth. This myth has many subthemes, and even opposing dynamics, but is not our subject here. Nonetheless, ignorance of these subtexts means that one lives an unconscious journey, or rather, is lived by unconscious powers.

Myth as tribal value system

Cultures as well as individuals live in service to values, not simply values that are conscious and rationally apprehended but values which operate unconsciously as well. The conscious values are embodied in a culture's ethical and juridical systems, its mores and its sense of identity. The unconscious values may be activated by propaganda and advertising, natural or political events, or collective intrapsychic dynamics.

For example, one could never explain the rise of a Hitler in economic and political terms alone. Some other dynamics were at work, as suggested by Jung in his writings on Nazism.[4] Such reasons included collective compensation for feelings of inferiority through such convenient fictions as racial superiority, projection of shadow contents, scapegoating and paranoid discernments of betrayal such as the *Dolchstosslegend*, or "stab in the back" conspiracy.

As Nietzsche suggested, it is amazing how bad reasons and bad music can sound so good when one is marching against the enemy.[5] Bad reasons and bad music divert one from the fact that a

---

[4] See, particularly, "Wotan" and "After the Catastrophe," *Civilization in Transition*, CW 10.

[5] "The Dawn," in *The Portable Nietzsche*, p. 91.

complex is in charge, a blood lust, a sinister value that one might be ashamed to confess by light of day. (Nietzsche was hauntingly prescient. Nearly a hundred years before the fact he also wrote, "Don't you smell the slaughter houses and the ovens of the spirit even now?")[6] Similarly, the American suppression of indigenous populations, the importation of slaves, and the subsequent institutionalization of racism are mythic enactments of the tribal shadow.

It may seem strange to call these collective movements mythic, but they are the enactments of charged imagoes, that is, value systems to which the psyche is bound, whether consciously or not. Even nations are moved by the invisible world, and the paradoxes of history, both personal and collective, are crafted by these dynamic forces.

If one objects that virtually any human pattern, product or value system could then be considered mythic, one would be absolutely correct. The point here is to make us more conscious of the fact that all values are psychically charged and that, so charged, they have a dynamic which almost always proves independent of ego control, and that the play of these value agents are the constituents of both personal and tribal history.

The aim is to become more attuned to the reading of the observable world, to become aware of the movement of the invisible. The other world, the invisible world, exists, and it is embodied in the visible world. History, and the individual, are the manifestations of these energies, the means by which the gods may become known in all their regal autonomy.

---

[6] "Thus Spake Zarathustra," in ibid., p. 288.

1
The Nature of Mythic Sensibility

How can the patterns of nature and the harmonies of the heart ever be plumbed, if not in the timeless movements of myth? Awash as we in the Western world are in material abundance, what links us to the spirit, connects us with the transcendent?

This dilemma of deracination, of severance from the tribal imagoes which linked our ancestors to cosmos, deity, tribe and self, has grown progressively apparent over the last four centuries. The scientific method, which separates subject and object and relies upon control, repetition and predictability, and the claim of kings and councils to determine the fates of all, leaves the modern adrift, bereft of any sacred narrative to point the way through forests of secular surrogates.

These primary shifts in human sensibility have brought benefit as well as bane. The sciences have improved our health and given us great powers of communication, production and transportation. The erosion of "divine right" has fostered democracy, and shifted the burden from monarch to citizen in a way which brings dignity and worth to the individual. At the same time, as Jung noted in 1936, "In the last analysis, most of our difficulties come from losing contact with our instincts, with the age-old unforgotten wisdom stored up in us."[7]

Instinctual wisdom may in fact be lost to the conscious mind, but in the vasty depths of the unconscious, the wisdom which nature embodies is never forgotten, and will manifest itself in pathology if otherwise denied expression.

---

[7] "The 2,000,000-Year-Old Man," in William McGuire amd R.F.C. Hull, eds., *C.G. Jung Speaking,* p. 89.

This history of history is well known and shall not be repeated here. But the problem of accessing the invisible world is always our core condition. To find a new slant in our time, as Barfield called it, requires a psychological attitude, the willingness to look beneath the surface to see what forces are at play and how they are internalized by each of us.

Much modern psychology is hardly worth the name, for it is not, as the etymology demands, a mode for the expression of "soul" (Greek *psyche*). Most modern psychology fractionates the person into behaviors, cognitions and neurology, treated in turn by modification, reprogramming and pharmacology. While these modalities can prove useful in specific situations, the larger question of meaning is frequently discarded in a failure of professional nerve and/or surrender to mass marketing. When the soul is not attended, what kind of healing can occur? Why should we go faster to some place, or learn more about some thing, when we have no idea who we are, or what values those bytes of information serve?

When we do not ask what the gods want—that is, what is the silent intention of those old autonomies of the soul—then we are living not only a superficial life, but also a deluded one. This insight is hardly new, but it requires a spiritual constancy in our lives lest we be carried away from ourselves by waves of acculturation. As the ancient Chinese text *Art of the Mind* observes,

> What man desires to know is *that* . . . . But his means of knowing it is *this* . . . . How can he know *that*? Only by the perfection of *this*.[8]

The *that* is the external world we would wish to know, but we may only know it by knowing *this*, our internal, highly individualized, way of knowing. If we do not know the *this*, then we are

---

[8] See Arthur Waley, *The Way and Its Power*, p. 47.

at the mercy of whatever *thats* the world imposes. The true evolution of our world is found less in Darwin, despite his great, useful metaphor, than in Jung, who provided moderns with access to the timeless realm of the psyche. The evolution of the world is found in the evolution of consciousness, the evolution of an awareness of the relationship between the individual and the autonomous world, between human sensibility and the godly autonomies.

Nonetheless, there is a malaise in the soul of modernism, a malaise which we sense in the daily newspaper, in our addictions and phobias, and in our troubled dreams. It is not naive nostalgia for an alleged simpler epoch, which we intuit in the disturbances of our time. Rather, as Jung suggests:

> Man feels himself isolated in the cosmos, because he is no longer involved in nature . . . natural phenomena . . . . have slowly lost their symbolic implications. Thunder is no longer the voice of an angry god, nor is lightning his avenging missile. No river contains a spirit, no tree is the life principle, . . . no snake the embodiment of wisdom, no mountain cave the home of a great demon. No voices now speak to man from stones, plants, and animals, nor does he speak to them believing they can hear. His contact with nature has gone, and with it has gone the profound emotional energy that this symbolic connection supplied.[9]

This mythic sensibility cannot be recovered—it is too long gone from us. We have become too conscious, which is to say, too split off from the instinctual nexus. Jung's last sentence is the critical point. The cosmos is an energy system of which we are a part. When we are no longer part of the living web of the world, then we are no longer either served or sustained by those connective energies.

Again, it is not that we can return to our original relationship

---

[9] C.G. Jung, ed., *Man and His Symbols*, p. 95.

with the world, but that we may be able to align the choices of conscious life with the deeper intentions of the psyche if we can reconnect with our buried mythological responses. As the psyche is the meeting place of the soul of the world and the soul of humankind, such realignment, while sparing us neither suffering nor death, will bring a deeper sense of harmony with the gods.

This is the whole point of working with dreams, after all. We do not know where dreams come from,[10] but we do know that if we track their mythopoetic images we open to the possibility of aligning the choices of consciousness with the intent of the soul. Such alignment, when we manage it, brings a sense of harmony and meaning. The alternative is service to split-off complexes or external norms, which brings neurosis. The discernment of one's personal mythology through the tracking of dreams is thus a work of mythopoetic attunement. In this fashion, at least for the moment, the old connection of which Jung spoke is reestablished and one is living a life expressive of the will of divinity.

There is a moving description by Jung in his autobiography, where he describes his deep connection to the energies of nature during his safari in Kenya. It bears repeating for its solemnity and depth.

From a low hill in this broad savanna a magnificent prospect opened out to us. To the very brink of the horizon we saw gigantic herds of animals. . . . Grazing, heads nodding, the herds moved forward like slow rivers. There was scarcely any sound save the melancholy cry of a bird of prey. This was the stillness of the eternal beginning, the world as it had always been, in the state of non-being; for until then no one had been present to know that it was this world. I walked away from my companions until I had put them out of sight, and savored the feeling of being entirely alone. There I was now, the first human being to recognize that this was the world, but who did

---

[10] Jung's useful fiction was the Self, by which he meant an autonomous ordering reality transcendent to the ego's frame of reference

not know that in this moment he had first really created it.[11]

The slow bestial rivers, the melancholic keen of scavengers, the pervading stillness: this moment is timeless; it is where the soul lives, whether ego is there or not.

As Jung is no fool, his comment at the end, his sense of co-creatorship of the world, is his recognition of the profundity of the partnership to which humankind is invited in the world. By bringing consciousness to the moment, and relinquishing the ego's usual compulsive commitments, Jung testifies to a *participation mystique* with the divinities. This depth of reality is present to us at all moments, but it is seldom present to consciousness. We cannot all walk away from the detritus of daily distractions onto such savannas of soul as Jung experienced in Kenya, but we carry this timeless dimension within us nonetheless. It has been the historic office of religion and tribal mythology to provide the numinous images which are capable of connecting us to such eternal moments.

Jung's statement is not an instance of anthropomorphic arrogance; rather, he is suggesting that such a partnership is a humbling responsibility, a sacred calling. He continues:

> Man is indispensable for the completion of creation; . . . he himself is the second creator of the world . . . without which, unheard, unseen, silently eating, giving birth, dying, heads nodding through hundreds of millions of years, it would have gone on in the profoundest night of non-being down to its unknown end. Human consciousness created objective existence and meaning, and man found his indispensable place in the great process of being.[12]

Our lives are an invitation to conscious reflection, a challenge to bear witness to a large symbolic drama which courses through history and through individuals. While the deeper intent of such

---

[11] *Memories, Dreams, Reflections,* p. 255.
[12] Ibid., p. 256.

intimations may puzzle, even frighten the ego, service to those great energies we call the gods obliges a more respectful relationship than that which we have more commonly lived.

It has been the historic office of the great religions to provide the images and community to support this mythic sensibility, this participation in the life of a larger order of being. For some this participation is still possible through their religious traditions and communities; for others the burden has shifted from sanctioned mace and miter to the privacy of personal journey.

Providing support for the individual's participation in a larger life is the chief task of depth therapy. As we know, the scope of most contemporary therapeutic practice is limited to symptom relief, behavioral and cognitive renovation, and pharmacological intervention. As useful as these techniques may sometimes be, in and by themselves they are superficial, considering that the deepest need of each of us is for meaning, for discovering spiritual points of reference, and for enlarged partnership in the making of one's life. Analytic psychology has been criticized for its alleged "crypto-religious" orientation. I would respond that precisely the deepening of spirituality, broadly understood, is the most cogent need of most of those who cross our therapeutic thresholds.

In incredibly varied ways, the religious problem lies underneath all of our pathologies, our symptomatologies, whether presenting as depression, addiction, relationship problem, grief, anxiety, or loss of direction. Further, Jung has been calumniated as, gasp! a mystic and a Gnostic. Either term refers to a person who has gained personal experience of the numinous, hardly a felony. We know that a person may attend a house of worship in order to avoid religious experience, even as one may enter therapy as an unconscious, apotropaic stratagem to keep the summons of the soul at bay. We know that much academic practice can be a form of talking about life in order to avoid living it. But surely such avoidance, hanging out until we die, so to speak, trivializes the soul. Surely coming to personal experience of the numinous is what life is all about.

A recent New Year's Day report of cosmological speculations predicts that if the universe keeps on accelerating at its present rate, subject to what astrophysicists call some "dark force," then,

> rather than coasting gently into the night, distant galaxies will eventually be moving apart so quickly that they cannot communicate with each other. In effect it would be like living in the middle of a black hole that kept getting emptier and colder.[13]

Blaise Pascal observed in the seventeenth century that the silence of these infinite spaces was frightening to him. What would he think to hear this article's conclusion, quoting astrophysicist Lawrence M. Krauss, about the endless widening of those spaces: "All our knowledge, civilization and culture are destined to be forgotten. There's no long-term future."[14] This reality, and the large metaphysical maze through which our species wanders, whether conscious, or intuited, lies underneath each visit to the therapist, haunts each house of worship, and finds gestural form in each of our daily, familiar pathologies.

It is not that depth psychology is meant to be a religious surrogate—quite the contrary. What arrogance that would be. The analyst is not a priest in mufti; he or she is, however, a servant of the god Hermes, the god of in-betweens, the god whose task it is to reveal divine intent. Depth psychology supports a person's engagement with the mystery of his or her journey, seeks to support that person in an encounter with the invisible world which does manifest in the course of a process undertaken with courage, integrity and consistency.

---

[13] Dennis Overbye, *The Houston Chronicle*, January 1, 2002.
[14] Ibid.

To focus on a person's presenting issue as "the problem," rather than a symptom of the problem, is an abdication of the healing profession's archetypal calling. To limit one's treatment plan to behaviors, cognitions and chemistry, is a failure of nerve, a refusal to open to the large questions which every life embodies. To treat the symptom alone is not only superficial, and counterproductive in the long run, but unintentionally insulting to one's own spiritual integrity.

The mythic sensibility is engaged whenever we are brought into relationship with depth, with the autonomous Other, be the Other a person, nature, or even some autonomous part of ourselves which demands the attention of consciousness. For some students of myth, this presentation extends the idea of mythic sensibility too far. Everything, almost, would then become mythogenic. Actually, everything *is* mythogenic as soon as it engages the ego and obliges its reformulation of meaning.

Thus, it is no hyperextension to say that one's own dreams are mythological, not only in the conventional sense that they often possess larger than life characters, numinous plots and darkening denouements, but because they reframe the ego's sensibility, whether consciously or not. I share the opinion that the dream is efficacious even when it is forgotten, ignored or rejected. It has occurred outside the sphere of conscious construction and has a numinosity which works its way upon us whether we know it or not.

As compensation for attitudes of consciousness, the dream is a dramatically charged fabric of values. If Jung is right, it has the intrapsychic effect of moving the ego, and even repositioning it, in the external drama of conscious life. Any encounter—with nature, with others, with the cosmos itself—has the potential for reframing our being. We are creatures of value, whether chosen by consciousness, and available to it in any moment, or not. We are mythological beings. Just as priest-poet Gerard Manley Hopkins once wrote that "the world is *charged* with the grandeur of God,"[15] so we live in charged environs. The kingdom is spread all over the earth, as Jesus suggested in one of the Gnostic gospels, and we do not see it.

The radical reframing of the ego's perspective, the denial of its fantasy of sovereignty, and its enlargement through encounters with that which it is not—all are spiritual engagements. It does seem peculiar to those raised in a narrow definition of belief, of creedal and dogmatic authority, that divinity may be found in such compelling moments. But those culturally accustomed to a personalistic deity, a sky-parent, so to speak, who watches over them and chastises them, brings them comfort and asks their worship, too often remain within constricted frames of reference. They suffer the diminishment of soul rather than its enlargement.

Job is an archetypal model of this dilemma. He is conventionally pious, well behaved, somewhat inflated in his superintendence of the piety of others, and only truly encounters divinity through his complete overthrow. Have not most of us had to learn in quite the same way the independence of those autonomous powers which shape our lives? Those who mediate the existential angst of our time by hovering about the precincts of orthodoxy, or, increasingly, fundamentalism, typically buy security at the price of authenticity, always remaining within a diminished frame of reference. Yes, it is true that the enlargement of our sensibilities most often comes from the distresses of the old sensibility, but precisely therein will be found our spiritual growth.

The flight from suffering, from consciousness, from personal responsibility in the face of the immensity of the space we traverse, is understandable; we are all familiar with it. But when we

---

[15] "God's Grandeur," in *The Norton Anthology of Poetry,* p. 855 (my italics).

examine the course our life demands, our own nature demands, and commit ourselves to it, then we are obeying the will of the gods, truly. Such obedience may bring little comfort or security, but it will bring a larger life.

A larger life is exactly what fundamentalism, and addictions, are designed to avoid. Nonetheless, as Jung wrote in a letter in 1960, "Anyone who falls down from the roof or ceiling of the Christian cathedral falls into himself."[16] Bearing the burden of spiritual or psychic transformation is more than onerous.

When it is not housed in the fundaments of simplistic belief systems whose chief purpose is apotropaism—that is, a defense against the spiritual realm—the timid ego will fall into various psychopathologies. The word "psychopathology" means, etymologically, "the expression of the soul's suffering." It is not for any of us to judge what twists and torments another's soul. It is our task, rather, to confront what our psychopathology otherwise enables us to avoid. Through our somatic symptoms, our avoidances, our addictions, we find ways to avoid the large and huddle within the small. It is no accident that Freud wrote a book a century ago called *The Psychopathology of Everyday Life*. One does not have to visit a prison or mental hospital to see the wounded soul; one finds it everywhere.

The "reading" of the daily world is more than enough task for us, tracking the endless drum of messages, or things in themselves, or red herrings, or voices of the gods. As William Matthews writes,

> Doesn't everything mean something?
> . . . [and how] can we bear the weight of such
> self-reference and such self-ignorance?[17]

---

[16] *Letters*, vol. 2, p. 569.
[17] "The Psychopathology of Everyday Life," in *The Norton Introduction to Poetry*. p. 157.

The nature of the mythic sensibility is found most in our curiosity, our capacity to ask "why"? and "what does this mean"? and "how am I to respond"? A good illustration of this process is found, not surprisingly, in Jung's autobiography, a portion of which recounts the difficulty of his midlife passage. Between 1913 and 1917 he was buffeted by inner forces just as the world was coming to know outer buffeting horrors in little towns called Verdun and Passchendael and Ypres. He feared being overwhelmed by the powers of his own unconscious; he feared being menaced by a psychosis, so powerful was the impact of those energies. One commentator has argued, wrongly to my mind, that Jung was in fact psychotic during this period.[18] He neglects Jung's own commentary on these experiences as well as the contained way in which Jung painted his fantasies—all in service to a dialectical conversation, what he called an *Auseinandersetzung*, in which the ego is responsive but does not abandon its standpoint. He believed that he was summoned by something divine to encounter experience which would be enlarging. As he describes, "I had an unswerving conviction that I was obeying a higher will, and that feeling continued to uphold me until I had mastered the task."[19] In short, he had to know what the gods wanted of him, what soul wanted.

Rather than seek mastery of the emotions that came his way, Jung sought to understand them by discerning what images they embodied. This next part is critical, for it represents the mythological sensibility, the capacity to see the movement of the spirit in material life.

> To the extent that I managed to translate the emotions into images—that is to say, to find the images which were concealed in the emotions—I was inwardly calmed and reassured. Had I left those

---

[18] See Paul Stern, *The Haunted Prophet*.
[19] *Memories, Dreams, Reflections*, p. 177.

images hidden in the emotions, I might have been torn to pieces by them. There is a chance that I might have succeeded in splitting them off; but in that case I would inexorably have fallen into a neurosis and so been ultimately destroyed by them anyhow. As a result of my experiment I learned how helpful it can be, from the therapeutic point of view, to find the particular images which lie behind emotions.[20]

This passage is very rich for our purposes. In the first place, Jung is noting that we can only relate consciously to those invisible energies when they become visible, that is, when they manifest as an image. Such images may be affective states, such as depression, or somatic states, such as our problems "stomaching" something, or dream images, or patterned behavioral images. Anything that infuses image with spirit may become available to consciousness.

Secondly, Jung notes that to ignore the images which rushed from his unconscious was to grant them sovereign power in his life. And thirdly, to split them off—repress them, or project them onto someone or something else—would thereby be to carry that intrapsychic split into one's dealings, to suffer what we have historically called a neurosis.

What Jung is talking about here is more than a personal crisis, and even more than a psychotherapeutic stratagem for healing, important as these may be. He is illustrating the mythological sensibility, the capacity to "read" the movement of spirit in the tangible world. He believed that not only was this personal work important to his effectiveness as a therapist, but that it was a responsible opening to some energy transcendent to the ego which wanted to express itself through him.[21] From a particular source which he found wise and knowing in himself, he came to

---

[20] Ibid.
[21] Ibid., pp. 178f.

affirm the autonomy of these images.

This conscious, deliberately respectful perspective differs from the psychotic condition that one sees illustrated, for example, in Sylvia Nasar's biography of John Nash, *A Beautiful Mind*. Nash's ego had been sufficiently weakened, most likely from a biochemical disorder, to the point that he could not differentiate the people in the room from his intrapsychic images of people in a room.

Jung is acknowledging the ineluctable power of image, and the necessary power of consciousness, to dialogue and produce enlargement. Repeatedly he says of his *Auseinandersetzung*, "Here is something else you didn't know until now."[22] He realized that he was dealing with the same sort of material he found in his psychotic patients at the Zurich Burgholzli Hospital. He writes:

> This is the fund of unconscious images which fatally confuse the mental patient. But it is also the matrix of a mythopoeic imagination which has vanished from our rational age.[23]

To clarify a bit further, the mythopoeic imagination has never gone away; it is no further from us than tonight's dream, tomorrow's projection of symbolic material onto another person, or the affective energy of the next day's headlines in our local newspaper.

What Jung found from this experience of dialogue was a sense of a transcendent source of wisdom and guidance in himself. This source he called the Self. Inevitably, from this dialogue comes personal enlargement. Additionally, he came to intimate that the Self was itself the recipient, or carrier, of energies transcendent to individual consciousness. While not confusing the Self with God, he nonetheless concluded that the Self is the channel through which we receive those energies that move stars and in-

---

[22] Ibid., p. 183.
[23] Ibid., p. 188.

dividual souls alike. From such a mythic sensibility came not the avoidance of suffering, of mortality, even of neuroses, but a wonderful richness of experience. As a result, Jung writes,

> It was then that I dedicated myself to service of the psyche. I loved it and hated it, but it was my greatest wealth. My delivering myself over to it, as it were, was the only way by which I could endure my existence and live it as fully as possible.
>
> Today I can say that I have never lost touch with my initial experiences. All my works, all my creative activity, has come from those initial fantasies and dreams which began in 1912, almost fifty years ago. Everything that I accomplished in later life was already contained in them, although at first only in the form of emotions and images.[24]

Jung's personal journey did help others to find access to what is large within and transcendent without. Those who once resided within tribal mythological systems, with their images of connection with divinity, with nature, with peers and with self, experienced both confirmation of personal locus and relationship to the transcendent. But today many suffer from the erosion of those connections and the sinking of the linking images into the unconscious.

Depth psychoanalysis, whether of culture or the individual, became necessary precisely because of the loss of tribal mythology. From such loss of mythic locus, the modern descended into despair, depression, addictions and mass movements—be they political, religious or materialistic—all representing an uneasy sojourning in a vacant world.

---

[24] Ibid., p. 192.

2
Beginnings

All peoples have their embroidered stories of First Things, of the Time before Time, of the First People, of the Ancients, the Wise Ones, the time when, out of the Nothing, out of the dismal disarray, out of the primal soup, out of the ouroboric chaos, came *cosmos*, a word which means "order."

Some of these accounts are solemn, some comic, some matter of fact, some provoke more questions than they answer. But every people has speculated about origins. Today we have accounts of our cosmos which utilize such metaphors as quarks and black holes; we learn that our solar system and a neighbor, Andromeda, are hurtling toward each other at something called warp speed, and in some billion or so years will collide and rip each other apart, perhaps fall into an implosive supermass, create another black hole and fling all we currently know of this world into a dreadful dark. (In the short term, it is probably still a good idea to pick up one's child at school, paint the house and pay our taxes.)

We also know something of causative factors which led to the concatenation of raw elements which are the necessary, dynamic constructs of matter as well as the dynamics of the whirling world we inhabit. It is now possible to construct a coherent theory of cause and outcome, as so many astrophysicists have done, which has no need for gods, for First Cause theory, or for teleology, revelation or eschatology. One need not posit a mindful deity, nor advocate absurdity and chance, to provide a coherent construct or picture of our given world. Nonetheless . . . there is a deep psychological need for explanation, for location in a context which provides some sort of answers to these questions, and which addresses what we metaphorically call the heart rather than the self-referential categories of mind.

The sentimentalist will fall into nostalgia for the old time religion, choose not to ponder such matters, or throw up his or her hands in dismay. The rationalist will seek heroically to live only with those artifacts of mind which are acceptable to the ego. Which one is not indulging in a matter of belief, which one is free of assumptions? Both positions are understandable, defendable, and matters of great speculation at best. Each remains essentially anthropomorphic, limited by the constraints of our mental instruments, and, as with most theologies and psychologies, tells us more about ourselves than what they seek to describe. The reading of the psyche, however, demands a different kind of rigor, and leads to a place in between the extremity of claims, between the either/or of which our nervous ego is so fond, and what Jungians like to call both/and.

Reading the world as it is presented to our sensibilities is of course fraught with the danger of misreading, of wish-fulfillment, of errors of interpretation, and of operating only within the limits of our time/space/societal constructs. That discipline called deconstructionism arose for very good reason. How easy it is to condescend toward another era's view of reality. Why didn't they see what we find so self-evident, we ask, forgetting that we stand on the shoulders of their errors as well as their discoveries and will no doubt appear slow to understand by our children's children. And yet, deconstructionism can get caught in its own limited frame as well.

While we may agree, echoing Kant, that all we say and do is a construct of our mentive instruments, colored by local culture and our own psychological limits, there are also energies which are autonomous, have a purpose of their own, however opaque we may be in their discernment. An argument for the existence of God does not mean that God exists; it means only that my mind can be seduced by circular logic. An argument for a model of the universe without reference to transcendent energies can also be seductive and have absolutely no bearing on reality. The French mathematician LaPlace replied to Napoleon's question about the existence of God that he had no need of that hypothesis in his system. Contemporary thought understands that his system was self-enclosed, and he unaware of openings to mystery which his colleagues in the next century would encounter.

The problem always comes back to the fact that we do not know what we do not know. We are not conscious of that of which we are unconscious. We do not apprehend that which lies beyond our instruments of apprehension. The wise, from Socrates to the present, know that they do not know, so all of life remains to them a mystery, a curiosity, which gets, as British astronomer J.B.S. Haldane once concluded, ever curiouser and curiouser.

Since we have to choose one example from the hundreds, nay thousands, available, let us focus for the moment on the one most influential in the Western world, the Biblical story of Genesis. Everyone knows the plot and the development; the denouement is still transpiring. The Judeo-Christian mythopoeic version seeks to answer the question *how* though never addresses what I consider the greater question, *why*. The Genesis story delineates a progressive imposition of order upon chaos, the void without form, and utilizes the metaphor of "language" to analogize how the deity construes the universe. Language as a metaphor is a recognition of a constitutive, intentional act. As a nomadic people, sometimes called the people of the Word, the Hebrews valued language not only because it transmits values but also because it is portable. When one is without home, one learns to value what one can carry along, hide from the intruder, and safely bring out when danger has passed.

So, God *speaks*, and it all happens, in progressive, intentional, and increasingly complex fashion. We are not told why, as is the case in many other creation stories. (To be God's entertainment, for example, or, in its Sumerian form, to be the laborers for the gods who wish to spend more time on the lofty cloudlinks playing whatever god-golfgame allows them to pass eternity.) Moreover, this constitutive power of language is passed on to the alleged apex of creation, humanity. (Might we detect some hubris here?) While we can look back on this story and see the prints of human intelligence and imagination at work, and, except for the literalist, acknowledge its mythopoeic invention, we still may take such a story and find what is durable, find what it tells us about ourselves.

Adam's task, to continue the naming, is to continue the ongoing act of creation. The Genesis metaphor implies the transfer of a divine power to a mortal creature. What are we to make of this? Whatever this world is about, it perforce obliges some sort of metaphoric partnership with the Unnamable Ones. Whether they pay any attention to us, or whether we have invented them, is hardly the point. The world as we find it is large, mysterious, intimidating, yes, but also open-ended, sometimes more open-ended than we can bear. And we have a stake in its exploration. When Jung realized that he was experiencing a primal moment on the African veldt, where the great herds drifted timelessly, he also knew that he was bringing consciousness to that moment, and bringing meaning to that world which would not otherwise have consciousness—the necessary precursor to meaning.

When Rilke, in the ninth *Duino Elegy,* asks the earth what it demands of us, he concludes that the earth asks to rise invisibly in us, and be embodied in our conscious apprehension. Yes, one could say that these are hubristic, anthropomorphic utterances, the product of deluded minds, but in the end we are obliged to undertake a partnership with the world in which we have been so inexplicably thrown. As Martin Heidegger notes, we are thrown into life (*entworfen*) and yet have the capacity for such consciousness as to be aware of our own impending annihilation (*Sein-zum-Todt*) in a way the rocks and trees and animals around us apparently do not.[25]

What does this tell us but of relationship, of partnership, of mutuality of world and consciousness?

While the world as it is is infinitely more complex than we can imagine, we are provided with the helpful tools of metaphor and symbol to move from the knowable world to the unknowable. If the poet compares the beloved to a flower, or analogizes the human life cycle with the seasons, we know full well what is intended. From this capacity for metaphor, symbol, analogy, we have the possibility through imagination of creating a partnership with mystery. The German word for imagination is *Einbildungskraft*, the power of creating a picture. The picture may come as an intentional act of mind, as these sentences are, or a gasp of aesthetic or horrified phenomenological experience which is embodied as image. The phenomenological appearance of such an utterance, such an image, is a de facto manifestation of something powerful about our nature. We are imaginal creatures; through images the world is embodied for us, and we can in turn embody the world and make it conscious. Such an act seems, in its generative, nominative and constitutive power—all godlike to me.

Note that in this metaphoric move we have not fallen into the either/or dilemma of insisting on the literal existence of such a story or said it is only metaphor, or even that it is only tribal metaphor.

Such a useful identification of the constitutive powers of the psyche, and the useful metaphor of saying may well delineate a

---

[25] See *Being and Time,* passim.

rich relationship to mystery and our partnership with it. Similarly, we find the compelling metaphors of dust, on the one hand, and *pneuma*, or spirit, on the other. While the equation of this fleeting flesh with dust has been a cliché of our world, the dialectic with spirit retains its use for us nonetheless. As Jung says,

> Spirit is always active, winged, swift-moving being as well as that which vivifies, stimulates, incites, fires, and inspires. To put it in modern language, spirit is the dynamic principle.[26]

As the dynamic principle, spirit is the dimension of psyche which embodies energy. If soul is the intentionality for meaning, for the wholeness of the organism, then spirit is the energy to go where desire leads. But Jung complicates the matter further:

> The hallmarks of spirit are, firstly, the principle of spontaneous movement and activity; secondly, the spontaneous capacity to produce images independently of sense perception; and thirdly, the autonomous and sovereign manipulation of those images.[27]

This is a challenging, heuristic sentence. Jung suggests that not only is spirit independent of ego control and, therefore, of consciousness most frequently, but that it operates independent of sensual stimuli, memory and literal experience. The so-called Romantics rebelled against the notion of imagination as decaying sensory impressions, an effort of the scientistic late eighteenth century to reduce mind/body/spirit to the metaphor of the machine. They understood imagination *(Einbildungskraft)* as the autonomous power of creating image. They moved imagination ahead of reason as the highest of human faculties. As useful as reason may be, it is surpassed by some creative demiurge, some

---

[26] "The Phenomenology of the Spirit in Fairy Tales," *The Archetypes and the Collective Unconscious,* CW 9i, par. 389. (CW refers throughout to *The Collected Works of C.G. Jung)*
[27] Ibid., par. 393.

autonomous *daimon* who conveys spirit from the gods into the realm of the human psyche, albeit often construed in baffling ways. Our dreams are a perfect example. When we want to know what the gods are thinking, we examine the investment of spirit in the artifacts of symptoms, in complexes, in patterns, in dreams. Each of those venues is a place for spirit to manifest.

Accordingly, we must offer homage to the powerful metaphor of spirit in matter, as Genesis depicts through the metaphor of divine breath blown into dust, *pneuma* infusing *materia*. Matter we are, body as machine, body as soul; and yet spirit we are, which infuses the material with energy. And the moment we think we have spirit under control, it slips away and invests in Shadow, darts forth in projection, is repressed only to rise up in stormy insurrection, lies buried under depression, but it is never, never absent, any more than the gods who have fled are really gone.

What we learn daily, as children and as seniors, is that our fleshly home is fragile, impermanent and perishing. As Yeats would have it for all of us, "Consume my heart away; sick with desire / And fastened to a dying animal."[28] And at the same time we long for the stars, make music, make love, make war, and knit neuroses from our fretted brows. The ubiquity of this image of fleshy spirit, or inspirited matter, remains compelling, remains our daily dilemma. At the moment of exultation, the twinge in the side is enough to pull us back to our earth. And yet, in the midst of dying, we may also create timeless song. Who is to say only one of those antipodes is true, and the other not? Both surely are, and the metaphor of Genesis holds.

Still another motif of Genesis stands the test of continuing relevance—the metaphor of the Other. Whether the Other is

---

[28] "Sailing to Byzantium," in M.L. Rosenthal, ed., *Selected Poems and Two Plays of William Butler Yeats*, p. 96.

the serpent, the opposite gender, Cain or Abel, the other is other, not us, and yet we all know deep down, the other is us as well. We embody Arthur Schopenhauer's puzzle of *Mitleid*, or empathy; how can we rise from the limits of our own sack of skin and self-interest, to feel the pain of the other? We can only do so, he argues, because we discern, imaginatively, that we and that other, underneath the differences, are one.[29]

And Percy Bysshe Shelley argues, in his *Apology for Poetry*, that the secret spring of empathy and sympathy is the imagination, the moral organ. Through imagination we are able to transcend the boundaries of the merely known, or barely known, and apprehend relationship to that which is other, even less known. And of course we recall John Donne's admonition that it is fruitless to send to know for whom the mourning bell tolls, for it tolls for us.[30] And let us not forget Jung's articulation of the shadow as that which we from an ego standpoint wish not to be, and yet that which is inescapably part of us as well.

The reclamation of the shadow is the task of the individuating person, for she or he is ethically charged with integrating the split-off parts into a comprehensive whole. The engagement of the other, which is so threatening to the primitive psyche, and is the source of fear, bigotry and most violence, is the ultimate moral challenge. In my Cain is my Abel, and in my Abel is my Cain. I am as frightened of my so-called goodness as I am of my so-called evil. The work of integrating, of dialoguing with, of respecting the energic powers of the Other, is an enduring task for each civilization and for each individual. The fate of the world hangs, precariously, on this capacity to encompass the other and dialogue with it.

---

[29] "On the Foundations of Morality," *Collected Works*, p. 293.
[30] "Devotions xvii," in Denis Donaghue, ed., *The Complete Poetry and Selected Prose of John Donne*, p. 12.

Thus, when we consider beginnings, we see that each of the creation stories will provide a different set of metaphors, each useful in its own way. Of the three metaphors identified here—the generative partnership, the unity/duality of matter and spirit, and the secret identity of self and Other—we see that we have been forced neither into the literalism of the nervous nor premature dismissal by the sophists. From the sorites of these dual metaphors we tap into something truly vital. By "thinking mythically," which is to say imaginatively, we apprehend a deeper relationship to the mystery, and to our partnership with it. To shirk this embrace of duality is to run from our proper work. As Marcus Aurelius noted two millennia ago,

> Must I grumble at setting out to do what I was born for, and for the sake of which I was brought into the world? You have no real love for yourself; if you had, you would love your nature, and your nature's will.[31]

It would seem to me that our nature's will, often lazy and avoidant, also created the metaphors which grace the limbs of story with tangible cerements. It is our nature's will that we be creatures of spirit as well as fading flesh, and that even our mortal tracking of these images leads us to the precincts of transcendence after all. The same nature which drowns in sloth and sleep, awakes to stir and tumult as well. The act of *creatio* is reenacted in every moment, whether we will or not. And when we do will imaginative engagement, we discover ourselves to be spiritual beings in the midst of a mortal masque after all.

---

[31] *Meditations*, vol. 1, p. 77.

3
The Archetype of the Child

Many wonder in our era why anyone should be interested in myth. Actually, Jung speaks to that question in a very direct way. In his essay on the archetype of the trickster, he writes that "all mythical figures correspond to inner psychic experiences and originally sprang from them."[32]

This is a most remarkable statement and merits examination. The psyche is manifold, synonymous with nature, and contains all possibilities. In me is the saint and the murderer, the ascetic and the lecher, the monastic and the bestial. When a figure shows up in popular culture, it is but the personification and dramatization of the energies of the psyche. As we recall, the energy of the psyche is invisible; so it is only rendered available to consciousness when it is made manifest in image. As Jung notes elsewhere:

> Myths are original revelations of the preconscious psyche, involuntary statements about unconscious psychic happenings, and anything but allegories of physical processes.[33]

So, what are those original revelations, and what can we learn from them?

To begin, there is the ubiquity of the imago of the child, which turns up so often in our dreams, in our waking life and in our fantasies. Too often we dismiss the image of the child as "nothing but" a memory of our own childhood. (Even if it were, surely that would be important to us psychologically, since the

---

[32] "On the Psychology of the Trickster Figure," *The Archetypes and the Collective Unconscious*, CW 9i, par. 457.
[33] "The Psychology of the Child Archetype," ibid., par. 261.

archaic images of childhood form so much of who we are. Jung pushes further into the image, noting that "the child motif represents the preconscious, childhood aspect of the collective psyche."[34] But what does this mean?

When we reflect on the image of the child, many associations come to us. Which one is central, which one explains our dream, which one can we explain? As we puzzle over this dilemma, we begin to recognize that all of them are important. Which outer child would a parent be willing to discard? All of them are important, all are loved, all have something unique to offer. Then we begin to tumble to the notion that the image is multifaceted, that it offers so many apertures which open to ever larger places in our experience.

So, what comes to mind when you think of child? Original, futurity, helpless, dependent, infantile, whole, unconscious, possibility, and so many more. . . . Which one is true? Surely all are truthful about something, are they not? Then we recognize the richness of the image, and the manifold ways in which it embodies meaning for us. The same multifoliate image, in this case the child, opens the door to a conscious engagement with so many possible entry points into our larger life. Let us consider a few.

The child as original form

The word "form" here is a useful metaphor. It is container that shapes, and it is shaping energy as well. If "the child is the father of the man," as Wordsworth avers,[35] then the original form is always present, seeking to shape energies in service to that archetypal idea. Just as Plato saw the basis of reality to be the Form or the Idea, so the metaphor of the child is an archetypal, formative process. As original form, it is origin, concept,

---

34 Ibid., par. 273.
35 "Ode: Intimations of Immortality," *The Norton Anthology of Poetry,* p. 551.

pattern, and patterning agent all at once.

When we think of the child as futurity, as possibility, as generative agent, we acknowledge the archetypal fundament of our being. Why do we have a tendency to ooh and ah at a baby? Why do we not look at it as a costly investment which will only end in death? Why do we not imagine the serial killer it might become? In the short story *Kiss, Kiss,* Roald Dahl tells of a poor Austrian woman who, after several miscarriages struggles to bring this helpless baby, this new investment in life, to birth. The reader is pulled into deep sympathy for her and is obliged to root for the survival of this fragile fetus, this helpless, weeping fragment of humanity, this child, this Adolf who will go on to be master murderer of the Third Reich. So, who or what are we found rooting for, then? For possibility, for renewal, for hope— despite all historical evidence to the contrary.

And yet life is renewal in the face of death and all history, and each child begins the journey once again. The child, each child, is the potential reinvention of the human race, for better or worse.

The lost child

The child is often apprehended as the original orientation to life: curious, joyful, spontaneous, all qualities of openness which make the journey possible. When we examine our adult selves, we commonly experience the absence of these qualities. We have become programmed, dulled, and find ourselves trapped in a web of reflexive responses. The very fragility of that child obliges its adaptation to the demands of its environment. Each adaptation, though necessary for survival, takes one further and further from the integrity of the child form.

So, frequently, the child seems lost to the adult—forlorn, betrayed, abandoned. Those qualities with which one was born and were intended by nature, have been subordinated to the *Realpolitik* of societal demands. While much sentimentality floats about the image of the child, the inner child, the lost child, still there is an existential truth to be served by this metaphor. As Jung observes,

> We can never legitimately cut loose from our archetypal foundations unless we are prepared to pay the prices of a neurosis, any more than we can rid ourselves of our body and its organs without committing suicide.[36]

We are separated from our ontological ground, and only therapy or transcendent experience, or occasionally relationship, offers hope of healing the internal split. In moments of spontaneity, in the act of dance perhaps, or sport, or spontaneous exuberance, we may revisit the original form for a brief while.

The child god

As the principle of futurity, the child is often the harbinger of the new, the compensation for the one-sidedness of the past. We think of Moses, imperiled in the bulrushes, Jesus evading the slaughter of the innocents, Gautama escaping the blandishments of his parent's pleasure palace, and many others, implying that the child arrives bearing the new dispensation while threatened by the old. Though he or she may suffer martyrdom or exaltation, emerging formative values will infuse the culture with new vision and a restorative energy. In many fairy tales, myths and religions, the values rejected by the collective are carried by gnomes, dwarfs, cabiri or other little creatures. They are scarcely seen at first by the collective ego, but in time they prove to embody values which are critical to the healing of the tribe. Smaller than small, they often prove to be bigger than big.

The child god is the agent of enlargement through reorienting values. Psychodynamically, the birth has actually occurred in the unconscious, symbolized by darkness, the cave, the manger. The

---

[36] Ibid., par. 267.

holistic motive of the Self, through the agency of the transcendent function, brings the new value to the threshold of consciousness. It may appear as a child in our dreams, a sudden visitation by our own lost child, or we may be brought to remembrance of the formative child through an actual outer child. Such a fragile vessel as a child is nonetheless the carrier of the future of the tribe.

Antithetically, in his book *Kali's Child*, Jeffrey Kripal traces the visionary experience of the nineteenth-century Ramakrishna to a vision of emptiness. Ramakrishna sees Kali, Goddess of Death and Passing Things, rise out of water, give birth to a child, and then eat it. What the ego found terrifying, the enlarged consciousness later realized was, "a relative moment in a flurry of mystical emptiness," concluding that "everything is empty."[37]

From this moment of passing things, Ramakrishna envisions the universe itself as a shape-shifting formative energy in which what the ego would call reality is passing, and what abides is the energy itself, often accessed through Tantric arousal rather than conventional forms of worship. (Thus, for example the famous Bernini statue of Teresa of Avila illustrates this orgasmic ecstasy through *coniunctio* with the Godhead.)

Here again one sees that the child motif opens the way to the possibility of deeper meaning than heretofore. When a child appears in a dream, it may very well betoken a possibility that already exists within the psyche but is denied or simply unconscious. This notion of the importance of the child archetype suggests that the germ of wholeness lies already within the psyche, and just as the literal child is driven by a genetic developmental plan, so the psyche unfolds the whole person through these intimations of the futurity of the child.

Yet, as we saw above, that whole is also bound for death as

---

[37] *Kali's Child*, p. xiii.

much as development. We are but one of those Ten Thousand Passing Things, a fact which the ego would deny, yet ironically the manifold ubiquity of denial is *prima facie* evidence of the psyche's extramaterial character. The psyche is timeless; the ego is time bound. As the organ of consciousness, the ego is constrained by schedules, finite numbers and dwindling days. As the organ of soul, the psyche is carrier of all, everything and nothing together, origin, end and purpose.

The child, in its unity and plurality, is as fit a symbol of this ontological mystery as any other. As symbol of plurality, we need remember that we do not have a single child within us, but a multitude, a virtual kindergarten of divergent energies, agendas and values. When consciousness is unaware of them, as most often it is, these parts are eminently capable of expressing themselves independently. In fact, under conditions of dissociation, entire spheres of personality may be dominated by one of these "children," as one often discovers with great embarrassment.

Within each of us is the child who would be hero and overthrow the demon of darkness. Also within is the dependent, lazy, infantile part which may show up to sabotage relationship, inhibit risk, keep us from growing up. Much New Age prattle about the "inner child" is an invitation to regression and sentimentality, a flight from the complexities of adult life. We all have experienced the lost child, the abandoned child, but how often do we recall that such separation is the necessary requisite to growth, to individuation? Similarly, the child mythologem is a spiral. We begin dependent, toothless, silly, and end dependent, toothless, silly.

Much richness of human experience lies contained within this single mythic image. To be sure, it arises out of our literal experience, but it is also something which arises from psyche to serve as a symbol of complexity. As Jung so profoundly summarizes the child mythologem:

It is a personification of vital forces quite outside the limited range of our conscious mind; of ways and possibilities of which our one-sided conscious mind knows nothing; a wholeness which embraces the very depths of Nature. It represents the strongest, the most ineluctable urge in every being, namely the urge to realize itself.[38]

And so, what is in the beginning is in the end, and present all along the way.

---

[38] "The Psychology of the Child Archetype," *The Archetypes and the Collective Unconscious,* CW 9i, par. 289.

4
The Parents

When we summon up the concept of *parent*, how quickly the experience of personal parent intrudes. How can we see beyond our complexes, beyond the limits of personal biography? Is there ever a time when the image may be witnessed with neutral affect? Probably not, for whatever one experiences of father or mother remains the central complex, that is, the primary, affectively charged imago of one's life. They were there at the beginning, they were the mediators of all experience with the larger world, and diffused or intensified the inherent trauma through which this life is experienced. Even when one seeks objectivity, pulls back from affect and solicits reason, does not the complex form the very lens through which one sees the matter?

Can we ever escape the Heisenbergian dilemma that the mere viewing changes the phenomenon? Is not our vision of Mum and Dad also a product of culture, and of gender roles which are undergoing redefinition as we speak? How can something be archetypal when it is so clearly bound to local culture and personal complex? Such musing is necessary, for we are obliged to try to make sense of this brief transit, however obscurely fleeting it may seem. And these fragile individuals assigned to us by Fate played a major role in the construction of our sense of self, world and relationships between them.

If, however, we reflect on father and mother as modes of expression, as personifications of energy, as teleological tasks, we open ourselves to the consideration of parents in general. And from those musings, we begin to discern how their effect in our lives emotionally colors our relationship to the gods as well. As Ezra Pound expressed it, "No apter metaphor having been found

43

for certain emotional colours, I assert that the gods exist."[39]

We are not talking now about your parents or mine; rather we are talking about personified notions, embodied energies. In any given family these energies may or may not be enacted by one actual parent or the other. When one has lived with an especially limited parent, or been orphaned, one may have lived without the expression of these energies altogether. In either case, the long-term task of the child *cum* adult is to witness and internalize those energies more consciously, or remain forever bound to Ixion's iron wheel of fateful repetition.

This task of identifying, perhaps overthrowing, the tyranny of the internalized imago is one of the chief tasks of therapy and all forms of healing. The unhealed person perforce reenacts these imagoes everywhere, and especially transmits the same patterns to his or her children. Accordingly, we cannot say that the parental imago is unimportant, that we outgrow it simply because our bodies have grown large, or that we can live without factoring its role into our complex lives.

The father imago

When we hear the nineteenth-century priest-poet Gerard Manley Hopkins say, "He fathers-forth whose beauty is past change: Praise him!"[40] we understand full well what he means by "fathering." When we seek to "mother" someone in need, we understand full well the metaphor. There may be terminological confusion, but there is no imaginal confusion.

Musing on the archetypal image of father leads one toward the creative or the destructive powers. The semen inseminates whether in the womb, the seminary, or the seminar. It is an activating principle. While it is not life itself, it must be lively to

[39] Cited by Roberto Calasso, *Literature and the Gods,* pp. 33f.
[40] "Pied Beauty," in *The Norton Anthology of Poetry,* p. 854.

create. It must be sprit enspiriting somehow, for spirit is the energetic principle of life.

As the hymn asks, "Breathe on me breath of god," or Shelley asks that the wild west wind enspirit his deadened psyche, so the masculine principle, whether in man or woman, is a lively, quickening, stimulating, enspiriting power.

We know from the story of Saturn who seeks the destruction of Chronos who seeks the destruction of Zeus, who himself is not a very likeable guy either, that fathers can also devour. As poet Sharon Olds writes of her saturnian father's abuse of her brother,

> . . . . his
> boy's feet crackling like two raw fish
> between his teeth. This is what he wanted,
> to take that life into his mouth
> and show what a man could do—show his son
> what a man's life was.[41]

She movingly suffers the fact that the archetypal energy which creates can also devour. Apollo's light and Saturn's darkness meet in life and form the ambivalent experience of each child. We recall Chronos who castrated his father, Ouranos, whose sperm, scattered on the salt-sea, produced sea-foam out of which came the goddess of love, Aphrodite (whose name means "born of the sea-foam"). From this fusion of violence and passion comes history, comes love, comes permutating gods, comes the duality of all life forms.

Recalling that a parental imago is a form of imaging various kinds of experience, and may or may not be tied to a specific gender, or a specific parental experience, we think of father also as protector, empowering agent, and ultimately that which is to

---

[41] "Saturn," in Robert Bly, James Hillman, Michael Meade, eds. *The Rag and Bone Shop of the Heart: Poems for Men,* p. 128.

be overcome in order to finds one's own authority. One finds virtually all tribes offering petitions for divine protection, as well as apotropaic rituals against judgment and punitive measures by an offended heaven—the beneficent or punitive father.

This duality continues in the theologies of contemporary life. Who shall stand by our side in our hour of need, the various psalms enquire? When one has no sense of personal or collective protector, one feels especially vulnerable, even naked, before a hostile universe. When one has had the gift of Father's blessing, or Father's example, or Father's sacrifice, one is privileged to feel worthy, empowered in the tasks of life, and part of a circle of connective affect. When one has not experienced these gifts as mediated through a personal father or surrogate, then one feels disempowered, and may spend one's life in search of ersatz authority, overcompensation through the power complex, or a life of unconscious disablement of one's own powers.

When a male or female therapist identifies such a lack in a client, the positive transference to the "masculine" within may serve to reparent, to activate those powers which lie dormant within us all. Reparenting means that the affirmation, the modeling, the encouragement and challenging we need from the father archetype may help compensate for what was missing in the actual biography of the patient. A positive transference is second best to the real thing, but it is no small gift and represents a liberation from the wounding of history.

Each person, male or female, is tasked with empowerment, namely the mobilization of energy in service to life, in service to overthrowing the regressive powers of the unconscious, with accepting the challenges of fear and loneliness. Regardless of the gender of the therapist, if he or she has access to such energies, they will be necessary and potentially healing to the patient. And, collaterally, what has not been activated in the therapist will only serve to fail the patient for the second time in his or her history.

Also associated with the father imago is the issue of authority. By whose authority do we live our lives, make our decisions, practice our professions, conduct our journeys? Authority as concept is neutral; in *praxis* it is always valenced. Any authority, no matter how benign and well-intended, can exclude its opposite and over time become oppressive. No child can ever wholly evolve into his or her own truth without finding an authentic inner authority. For this reason, the individuation process obliges some form of overthrow of the external authority, whether modeled by the personal parent, the broader culture, or the resident tribal deity.

Much sentimentalization of the family and of tradition overlooks the fact that individuation obliges some revolution, some transcendence of external authority to come to one's internal authority. Did not Thomas Jefferson, himself a landed burgher and patriot, say that periodically the tree of liberty is to be watered by the blood of its patriots? Do we not recognize the truth in Freud's archetypal drama of the primal hoard which must slay the old king to bring about the new generation? Is not Nietzsche correct when he says that the student ill serves the teacher who does not surpass him?

These revolts against authority are the only way in which a new authority may be found. It begins with a child learning to keep something secret, to protect some part of the psyche which needs security and solitude in order to live. It takes form in the many experiments of the child, in the revolt of adolescence, in the need to move out of the house. And when these separations are not achieved, the vitality of the personality is sapped, the life which is meant to flourish withers. No matter what security is offered by staying on the home range, within the protection of a perceived authority, the gift of the developed person to the world is denied though this failure of individuation.

The angst-driven search for external authority through fundamentalism is a flight from personal growth and development, an abdication of the summons to individual life. The gain of security comes at the expense of the varieties of life's experiment, of which we are the wayward but necessary carriers.

Thus, the father imago is, as are all archetypal energies, double edged. It empowers and/or castrates; it authorizes and/or tyrannizes; it protects and/or crushes. Whenever we are dealing with issues of personal authority, whenever we are dealing with our own capacity or impotence, whenever we are serving the *imago Dei* or questioning its relevance to our actual life, we are dealing with the father archetype in all its many forms. Whenever we seek the protection or destruction of another; whenever we impose our authority on another; whenever we pass on a message of empowerment or disempowerment, we are fathering, regardless of our gender or conscious intention.

"Father" is a metaphor for a distinct energy which exists in the cosmos and in each of us as well. Father is an inescapable half of a divine pair.

The mother imago

"Mother" is a metaphor for another kind of energy, with multivalent forms. It may be transmitted to us via our personal mother, left as a void if she was wounded, or sought for in her many surrogates, from the arms of the eleemosynary beloved to the *alma mater*, to any encompassing ideology which makes one feel at home on this whirling speck of dust.

The archetype of mother is both the source of life and source of death. She is home and, sometimes, even journey, whenever we are courageous enough to accept that our journey is our home. She is multileveled: personal parent, grandparent, maternal goddess, or even social structure which invokes awe, desire for connection, and some form of nurturance or sustenance. She is seen in her ambivalent forms as a goddess of fate, as the Russian Baba Yaga, with her head that turns back and forth at every juncture, inviting success or destruction. She is the goddess of death as the Hindu Kali, and, as Dylan Thomas phrased it, "the force that through the green fuse drives the flower,"[42] which also destroys. The same Great Mother who has given us life is speeding us toward extinction, and all in service to a great mystery which befuddles the conscious mind, terrifies the heart and stirs the soul. As the oldest of mythic cycles, the "cycle of sacrifice," we celebrate her beneficence at the dinner table even as we are being eaten by mortality's mordant mole. Eat up, enjoy and be eaten.[43]

Why does the mother play such a profound role? The obvious answer is that we come from her, are nursed by her, sustained or oppressed by her, and, generally, her ubiquity during the most formative phase of our personal psychology necessarily leads to a huge imprint on the psyche. After all, she is not only immense and necessary, she is both behavioral and values model, and mediator with the larger world, all at the same time. The core message that we all receive, namely that the world is big and we are not, that the world is powerful and we are not, is either given a moderated valence or a reinforced valence as we internalize our experience of her. As she is, so our world is, and thereby much of our life is preprogrammed. And yet, as important as this personal engagement is, Jung reminds us that the personal mother is but the carrier of even larger energy:

> I attribute to the personal mother only a limited etiological significance. That is to say, all those influences which the literature describes as being exerted on the children do not come from the

---

[42] "The Force That Through the Green Fuse Drives the Flower," *Collected Poems*, p. 10.
[43] For an extended discussion of this motif, see my *Tracking the Gods*, pp. 54ff.

mother herself, but rather from the archetype projected upon her, which gives her a mythological background and invests her with authority and numinosity.[44]

Jung is surely correct, and not so correct. Certainly he "read," or "misread," a great deal about the world from the experience of his personal mother. Given her bouts with mental instability, Jung thought of the word "unreliable" when he thought of women, and perhaps therefore of life itself. At the same time, we can see how both the personal data and the archetypal extension flow in and from the same parent, and in both directions.

The purpose of this discussion is not, finally, to deal with our particular mother or father complexes. Although that is rich work indeed, it is another project for another day. As Jung notes:

> Our task is not, therefore, to deny the archetype, but to dissolve the projections, in order to restore their contents to the individual who has involuntarily lost them by projecting them outside himself.[45]

In other words, what is projected is always some part of ourselves, though we do not know it in the moment. The collapse or erosion of a projection may feel like a disappointment, even a defeat, but it is an enormous opportunity for self-knowledge.

"What part of myself, what energy, what unknown task, did I project on to that person or situation?" Such work is necessary for consciousness and for individuation.

As we live our lives through projections, we are not unlike a person stumbling through a haunted house, brushing the cobwebs away, never being able to see or discern clearly. Even when we are aware of some etiological influence, the staying power of such energy is immense. The poet Rilke said that despite many engagements, marriage and affairs, he could not love women be-

---

[44] "Psychological Aspects of the Mother Archetype," *The Archetypes and the Collective Unconscious,* CW 9i, par. 159.
[45] Ibid., par. 160.

cause he could not love his mother. How sad to be kept from openness to such a huge part of life, especially when one is partially aware of the source of the discomfiture! Staying stuck in such a generalized projection is, in the classic sense of the term, tragic, for it binds the person to the wheel of repetition without respite or repair.

The son's enmeshment with the mother

The boy who believes he is the apple of his mother's eye will feel invincible, at least until life corrects this view. He will feel magically full of himself and may in fact do large deeds in the world. He may have learned from her to differentiate his feeling function and achieve great sensitivity to the nuances of relationship. He may have a finely tuned aesthetic sense, a capacity for greater self-expression.

Often, however, the boy has felt himself to be his mother's agent in the world. He is charged with making her life meaningful to her, with making her proud of herself. In fairness to many mothers, historically the societal constrictions placed on women which inhibited their own unfolded lives, made it all the more obligatory that she see herself through the achievements of her husband or son. Often that same son had to carry another unfair burden. As she was dissatisfied with her relationship with her husband, the son became scapegoat for the denigration of things masculine, or the repository of her hopes, fears and ambitions.

One analysand announced his psychological task in our first meeting this way: "I want to learn to become an ordinary person." This man had carried the weight of his mother's ambition for six decades. He had had to carry her to higher levels of society than his father was capable. He showed me his letters to her when, as an adolescent, he wrote from camp. Each was filled with lists of his accomplishments and agenda for more glory. Naturally, he married a woman who was equally expectant, needy and demanding. While he had achieved notable things, he had also been burdened, perhaps even diverted into a career not his own choice, by the weight of being her extraordinary son. We can see that learning to be "ordinary" was nothing ordinary for him. Learning to trust his own voice, his own instinctual direction, contributed to healing the demonic power of the de facto mythology of his life: to be mother's extraordinary boy.

As long as his psyche unconsciously served the mother's ambition, he was a prisoner. Recognizing that much of his life had been an extension of her ambitions was at first the source of much anger, but in time he learned the necessity of sorting through the skein of inner voices to find that which was his own. This sustained sorting through is obligatory for any of us in order to open the possibilities of genuine choice.

The power of the mother complex to affect the archetypal ground of the son cannot be overemphasized. By way of summary, we should recognize at least the following patterns.[46] When the mother holds too much sway in the boy's development, he is inclined to reflexively transfer that power to his partner, leading in its more pronounced form to the so-called virgin-whore complex. He has trouble sorting out his sexuality from the mother domination, unconsciously transferred to his partner, and so splits it off and is able to share it only in the dark side of his personality. Sharing his sexual life with his partner is like approaching the mother, so he is obliged to look as far in the opposite direction as he can. Or he may have unconsciously solved his dilemma by becoming a priest, philosopher or artist who, by putting his eros "up there," in the air as it were, is spared from mother's criticism or interference. This Jung called

---

[46] For a more extensive treatment of these issues, please see my *Under Saturn's Shadow: The Wounding and Healing of Men*, especially the chapters "Dragon Dread" and "Father Hunger."

the *puer aeternus* (eternal child) syndrome, which manifests psychologically as a man remaining an adolescent by being in service to the mother.

A variant of this issue is the Don Juan, always in search of the perfect woman. He idealizes each new find, quickly discerns her flaws, then denigrates her and moves onto the next conquest. His search is doomed, not only because he is enmeshed in the maternal material, but because his quest will ultimately bring him only to emptiness. In fact, he met that total woman once, and she was mother.

By far the preponderance of men, unconscious of the power of this archetypal contamination, avoid women, seek to control them, or compulsively strive to please them through the distorted lens of the mother complex. They are unable to see the individual for who she is; they see her only through the mythographic lens of their own personal history. Their partner is a giant, psychologically speaking, for she has received powers and numinosity transferred to her that replicate the original matrix of mother and son. No wonder so many relationships go awry, given the distortions they embody.

How sad it is that so many men remain trapped in this frozen history, controlled by a mythological script which, without conscious effort, can only repeat itself. No matter how much they hate or fear or idealize women, they still live in service to mother, whether they know it or not. No matter what mountain they have climbed, they have served her. Dark, unconscious mother, always near, on soft feet treading through the background of his desperate, driven life.[47]

---

[47] In his 1938 essay on the mother complex ("Psychological Aspects of the Mother Archetype," *The Archetypes and the Collective Unconscious,* CW 9i, pars. 162ff.), Jung attributed homosexuality to the preponderance of the mother complex in a boy's life, a speculation which does not stand up in the face of modern biological and genetic findings.

Whether the result of the power of this hidden mythologem is idealization, as in the courtly love tradition—the *Minnesingers* and troubadours—or sentimentality, as in much country music, or denigration of the feminine energies, the average male lives out a deep mythological pattern which estranges him from life and from himself. The most subtle and most sinister form this pattern takes is in his alienation from his own body, from his inner world, and from the possibility of intimacy with himself. His life, then, is one long estrangement. As Albert Camus begins *L'Etranger*, "Mother died today, or was it yesterday."[48] We marvel at the character's profound estrangement from feeling, from any sense of grounded identity, but, as Camus no doubt intended, his number is legion, and his tribe is everywhere. It is a mythological script which is in service to history, not to the advancement of life.

The daughter's enmeshment with the mother

The most positive mothering influence for a daughter today is found in the model of a mother who discerns her own deepest desire and follows its will in and through the world. No matter what her choices, such a blessed daughter will feel the freedom and the permission to be herself in all her spheres of choice.

The negative myth which the mother can engender is to usurp her daughter's life, secretly co-opt it to serve her own needs. Some of the ways in which this negative mythos can be seen are as follows. The daughter may be swamped within her mother and lose all sense of initiative, capacity to choose, and permission to go her own path. If the mother has defined herself only in her mothering role, she may tacitly compel her daughter to the same destiny.

One patient, who had a child at seventeen, was devastated

---

[48] *The Stranger*, p. 1.

when her daughter went away to school. She had no clue as to how to live her own life. Fair enough, and fair material for analysis. But her daughter immediately got pregnant, needed to work, hired her mother to raise her child, and the mother just as quickly stopped therapy. It turned out that she was the third generation to have a child as soon as she could.

Much sentimentality can cloak the fact that there is a brutal suppression of life in this apparent nurturing of life. Jung puts it this way:

> Though continuing "living for others," [they] are, as a matter of fact, unable to make any real sacrifice. Driven by ruthless will to power and a fanatical insistence on their own maternal rights, they often succeed in annihilating not only their own personality but also the personal lives of their children.[49]

A third pattern is the daughter's resistance to her mother's power in her life. She will become anything but her mother, anything but what her mother's designs intend. She is, of course, still dominated by this power, whether conscious or not, and is determining the course of her life by someone else's life.

And lastly, one sees the daughter reacting to the power of her mother imago by overidentifying with the father or with masculine energies. She will range from an eternal daddy's girl, or *puella,* to a career-driven executive who cuts herself and others no slack. She would rather be with men, be recognized as one of them, than explore her feminine nature. For her, whatever she thinks may be feminine feels contaminated by the mother material, but in so living her life she remains a little girl and not a woman, no matter how accomplished she may be. She is highly prone to fear of aging, suffers psychosomatic anxieties, and feels her hold on life is delicate and fragile. Like the boy who carries

---

[49] "Psychological Aspects of the Mother Archetype," *The Archetypes and the Collective Unconscious,* CW 9i, par. 167.

his mother's secret animus life, this woman flees her mother and thereby also flees herself. If she fights her father, she may at least claim herself; if she fights her mother, she may split off from something she needs to find in herself as well.

It may seem that we are loading up poor Ma and Pa with too much mythic weight, and so we are. They are, after all, only someone else's child all the while. They are finite, fragile, and as fraught with fear as any child, even though to the child they are giants who possess magic powers and infinite wisdom, who omnipotently bestride the great gulf of the immense unknown which looms before every child. Each parent, as Jung reminds us, is "deserving of love, indulgence, understanding, and forgiveness."[50]

Again, to think mythically is to discern what these issues mean, what energies are embodied, what tasks identified. What is incarnated in myth—our complexes and neuroses are dramatizations of embedded myth—helps make the invisible world more visible. In each of the parents one sees both form and dynamism, that is, a template for influence, and a driving core which takes it toward some sort of fulfillment.

Each of us has a so-called masculine task, and each of us has a so-called feminine task. If our minds call up too literal a picture of these tasks, we may be ensnared either in imitation or adolescent rebellion. If we see them as the twin embodiments of life's forms and dynamisms, we gain an enormous sense of the archetypal task before us. Our summons is both *to be* and *to do;* it is to nurture and to define; it is to be at home and to journey. If historically these energies and these tasks were delimited to specific genders, then everyone suffered an oppression of some vital part of themselves. Still, even for those who live in a deconstructionist age and can discern the mark of local time and place

---

[50] Ibid., par. 172.

on such categories as gender, the ancient tasks remain to be lived in their timeless ways.

At the same time, we must acknowledge the power of those fractile mythologies Jung called complexes, clusters of experiential energy, interpretations, value systems, provisional identities, reflexive strategies which together bind one powerfully to the past. As one internalizes the experience of the personal mother or father, so one has a tendency to generalize through behavior and attitude. We all suffer from the fallacy of overgeneralization, mistaking our powerful, formative experiences for the whole and, because of our predispositions, tending to find them confirmed in subsequent experiences.

Little do we know that we set up these repetitions because of the splinter mythologies that each complex represents. Little do we know that we are compelled by unconscious fictions, that is, constructs which are derivative rather than rising out of each unique experience life brings us. To map the psychological terrain of a person is to engage in mythographology, to depict the various scripts which each fragment of the whole embodies. We serve mythology all the time, whether we know it not. The manifold forms of the child, of father, of mother, and also our relationships to them, play out in the schemes and fantasies of everyday life.

5
The Hero Task

What is the hero today? What myth serves? Are there heroes in a world which increasingly dwarfs the individual?

In the 1930s William Butler Yeats stirred no little criticism in his decision to include none of the World War I poets in the *Oxford Book of Modern Verse*. In the introduction he explained his decision to exclude such popular poets of the time as Wilfred Owen, Isaac Rosenburg and Siegfried Sassoon by saying that, in an age of tanks, poison gas, aerial bombardment, the Maxim machine gun, and the horrors of the trenches,

> Passive suffering is not a theme for poetry. In all the great tragedies, tragedy is a joy to the man who dies; in Greece the tragic chorus danced. When man has withdrawn into the quicksilver at the back of the mirror no great event becomes luminous in his mind.[51]

Yeats, great as he was, here offers, I think, too narrow an understanding of the heroic. He sees the leveling of modern democracy, the depersonalization of bureaucracies, as the replacement of the noble with the ordinary. Rather than expire on some contested, elevated rampart, we die ordinary, squalid deaths: "Some blunderer has driven his car on the wrong side of the road—that is all."[52] The tenor of our time is, in Yeats's view, depersonalization and anonymity.

But what, really, is the myth of the hero, when separated from the hyperbole of film and legend? What role does it play in our daily lives? What mythologem is at work?

In sum, the hero is a name for, a designation of, a personifica-

---

[51] Yeats, ed., *The Oxford Book of Modern Verse*, p. xxxiv.
[52] Ibid.

tion of, a certain energy and intentionality which lies within us all, all the time, though we may have very uncertain access to it.

The hero mythologem is a personification of the energy necessary to serve life's transpersonal agenda, especially its developmental sequences. We are brought here, and every cell in our body knows this, to become, to flower, to flourish. At the same time, there are enormous forces which oppose this development.

In his wonderful parody, "The Night Sea Journey," John Barth portrays a central character who swims upstream against increasing odds. He is the sole survivor of this perilous journey. His comrades failed and fell long before in the various carnages of history. He struggles to make sense of his journey and runs the theoretic gamut from pietistic paeans to paternalistic deities to Darwinian metaphors of survival of the fittest. All he knows is that he swims upward toward his goal, his Valhalla, his appointment with destiny.

The reader is amused finally to recognize that the speaker is a single human sperm who is solitary yet carries the code to recreate the whole story of the world again. Against all odds, one sperm alone survives the journey to unite with the egg and begin the old, old story anew. Just as Jung speculated that if we were to all perish but one, our whole story would be recreated, for the story is implicate within our codes, within our psychic structuring processes. Any one of us would recreate the world, not just from memory, but from the common dream which is our spiritual heritage, the hard wiring in our brains and chromosomes.

The forces that oppose our hero task are awesome and obvious. We end, all, in annihilation. But the forces within are even more awesome and humbling. They are embodied in our fears, our desires for comfort and abundance, our longing to drown in our origins, to fall back into unconsciousness, to end this fearsome journey of uncertain ends and constant suffering.

Just recently I drove through the Wind River Canyon of

Wyoming and observed the various strata of cliffsides there, some going back 300 million years, moving and shifting long before our species even walked the planet. How we have survived as a species for these many millennia is a remarkable and implausible story, and how astonishing, in addition, that each of us daily renews the journey toward whatever end awaits.

The hero task is apparent in the humblest of lives, especially in those who rise wearily and go off to demeaning labor to support their families. It is seen in the willingness of any person to sacrifice creature comforts, narcissistic interests, personal agendas on behalf of a larger value. We do not customarily accord these persons hero status, but their acts renew the world each day, redeem it even, as a place of enduring value. In our narcissistic and superficial society, we transfer our own yearning for the heroic onto others, grant such status to movie stars, sports figures, celebrities of all kinds, all of which is a measure of how dismal is our understanding of our own daily summons to the task of individuation. We are all, every day, faced with death, depression and despair. Whoever rises to do what must be done, does a deed for us all.

Joseph Campbell was right to bring the hero to our attention, identifying him or her as an agent for bringing new values to the tribe, modeling large action.[53] But we would really miss the point if we did not see that such a task lies within the summons of us all. In the face of the overwhelming depths that intimidate, the immensity of the spaces around us, and the hosts of ignorance and bigotry who oppose us, who would not long for some hero to carry the day and spare us our moments of critical choice?

Anyone who is even semiconscious will be aware of many moments of what is called cowardice by the crowd, especially those who can easily scapegoat their own fears on an available

---

[53] See *The Hero with a Thousand Faces.*

target. Yet each person quick to label others has many moments of personal intimidation, of turning away, of being undone by fear and its many forms of paralysis. Only when we can acknowledge such fears and shortcomings as universal, can we relieve the scapegoat of his burden and assume it for ourselves. In his play *Galileo*, Bertholt Brecht has one character say, "Unhappy is the land that has no heroes." A second character replies, "Unhappy is the land that needs a hero."[54]

Brecht's frame of reference is of course more political than personal, for his aim was to show that Galileo was, like us, intimidated by the Church's instruments of torture, even as he dared to think the unthinkable about this planet and its place in the greater cosmos. The aging astronomer had every reason to be conquered by fear (and Brecht wants no Aristotelian heroes, only common persons of common sense), but still Galileo could not stop his imagination and his keen mind from drawing new, risky conclusions. Thus he was a hero of culture. He stretched the limits of our imagination.

Few of us have led lives more tortured than Beethoven, but he, too, pushed the limits of sound and created a new loom for music. The list goes on. Each one of them facing fear, facing rejection, sometimes even persecution, and yet answering an inner call to witness the truth of their own experience. Such is heroism for the culture, and a fit model for each of us.

We are not here to ape another's life or values. The *imitatio Christi* is found not in emulating the Jew of Nazareth, or walking about with a begging bowl like little Gautamas in hope of instant Buddhahood. Nothing will take one further from the truth of those religious heroes than slavish imitation. Their individuation task has already been accomplished. Our duty is to risk living our lives as fully as they risked living their truths.

---

[54] *Galileo*, p. 99.

This redefinition of heroism puts things in a different light. The hero's task is inescapable. It is renewed every day, perhaps every moment. None of us is up to heroic choice and action all the time, or perhaps even most of the time. But we each have an appointment with ourselves, though most of us never show up for it. Showing up, and dealing with whatever must be faced in the chasms of fear and self-doubt, that is the hero task.

The ambivalence one feels toward this task is understandable, for it always means leaving a known, rather more secure place for a less known, presumably less secure place. World literature is fraught with illustrations of this reluctance. The Biblical story of Jonah and the whale is a particularly familiar illustration of this archetypal pattern. He sought to flee his summons to individuation and ended up in the belly of the beast. What is that but a symbol of a regression into the warm darkness of the unconscious? Yet, sometimes the teleology of the soul is such that it will oblige transformation, whether we will it or not, and the hero archetype is the primal metaphor for that channeling of libido in service to development.

We often find ourselves driven into this next new place, pulled out of security and satiety into a dangerous but developmental agenda. The symbol of the summons of Jonah by Yahweh in the Bible is not unlike the summons of the ego by the Self. In tribal mythology, this process has often been described as the night-sea journey, the night suggesting the unknown, the sea suggesting the unconscious, the journey suggesting the transformation of libido. The *mare nostrum* is, after all, our sea, our "mother"; we swim such an inner sea no matter where we travel.

Many a mariner has gone under in those dark waves.

The sea is choked with would-be heroes who have drowned. For every knight who slew a dragon, ninety-nine predecessors failed. Yet, whether forward or backward, both paths lead to death. The way back is the death of a person's potential through regression, sometimes even resulting in the annihilation of the personality, as for instance in a psychosis.

Curiously, the nearly universal incest taboo is an unwitting recognition of this danger. Psychologically, incest means to commingle with the same, rather than be fertilized by the new. Just as it may be deadly at the genetic level, so the refusal to engage the foreign "other" is a commitment to stagnation. Fundamentalism is a flight from the foreign value, a capitulation to fear, and therefore feeds on itself and is unconsciously incestuous. Such self-circulation can only breed monsters in the end.

The great public interest in pedophilia today too often results in admonitions to refrain, as if it were simply a matter of behavioral choice. However heinous the abuse of a child is, the real dilemma must be probed where the libidinal development is stuck, in an early developmental place. The perpetrator is fixated in an incestuous libido cycle in which he or she is seeking to reconnect with an earlier aspect of his or her history. The body and the culture have pulled the person beyond his or her developmental achievement. As this fixation is often linked to a trauma at some early level, we can see how difficult it is for that person to be attracted to someone more inwardly evolved.

The same issue may also operate in adult sexuality, as the phrase *la petite mort* suggests. To seek "the little death" in the arms of the beloved is of course inviting and seductive, and falls short of the larger exchange of pleasure and meaning with the autonomous other which adult sexuality would ask of us. Similarly, the ubiquity of pornography, accounting for more internet traffic than any other category, is a refusal to engage the absolute other as an equal. The playboy is, finally, a boy and not an adult. When one is bound to the world of fantasy, one is still subordinated to the mother complex, whatever one's gender or station in life. The paradox is that the fantasy is a compensation for the task unaddressed by conscious life, and, moreover, allows one to retreat ever further from it.

More abstractly, the capacity to relate to the other is enlarging intellectually and conceptually as well. Ethnocentrism, which is found in all cultures, is a form of incest as much as fundamentalism. It is a flight from the dialectic which others invite and a regression to the familiar. This duality of desire is found in all human relationships, individual and collective, and at all stages of our lives. It may seem strange to the reader to consider these matters as contextual dimensions of the hero archetype, but they do represent arenas in which the summons to growth, the demand to overthrow the regressive powers of the unconscious, are encountered on a daily basis.

Nonetheless, the way forward also obliges death, the sacrifice of the old ego so that enlargement may occur. As the lobster splits its skin, annually leaving its comfortable home for a more capacious housing, so we are summoned repeatedly to death and concomitant growth. How vulnerable the lobster is between housings, and how vulnerable we are between mythological identities. Often the chief service of therapy, or a good friend, during those in-between times, is to hold the fragments together long enough for the new myth to form.

A person caught between myths, or a culture between myths, is in peril, but that is the only place to be when nature, divinity or the soul commands. One person said to me, while going through abandonment and disorientation, "I could never understand the idea of resurrection before this. I now understand that I had to die in order to come to myself. I was so identified with my marriage, with my parenting role and comfortable life that I didn't know I had not yet come to be myself."

Such a person does not choose to die. Her old myth was dying on her. That mortal transit is chosen by the gods, by fate or by the Self, yet such a person receives a blessing from the experience by coming to a new sense of self, a new mythology. That is the outcome of the Jonah story. Such a person has lived the hero journey whether conscious of it at the time or not. The hero task here is the redemption of the individuation process from all who would carry its burden in a provisional way. It is not of course that anything was intrinsically wrong with a marriage role, with parenting or with possessions; but it was that each of them subtly seduced the spirit away from the challenge of growing up and out of the sleep of childhood. Jung explains:

> Even if a change does occur, the old form loses none of its attractions; for whoever sunders himself from the mother longs to get back to the mother. This longing can easily turn into a consuming passion which threatens all that has been won.[55]

The "mother" to which Jung refers here is of course the mother complex in its generic form, the desire to be taken care of and protected which, understandable as that may be, results in the abrogation of individuation. Refusing to grow up is not just a personal decision; it affects all those who must deal with us and our unfinished business, and it wounds the world by removing our full humanity from its intended contribution.

It may seem a stretch to associate fundamentalisms and infantility as well as the overburdening of intimate relationship with neediness, but what they all have in common is the triumph of fear, of laziness, of the lethargic powers of the instincts and the unconscious. The capacity to sacrifice these regressive longings stands at the heart of true religious and psychological heroism. As Jung writes in a challenging fashion:

> It is not possible to live too long amid infantile surroundings, or in the bosom of the family, without endangering one's psychic health. Life calls us forth to independence, and anyone who does not heed this call because of childhood laziness or timidity is threatened with

---

[55] *Symbols of Transformation,* CW 5, par. 352.

neurosis. And once this has broken out, it becomes an increasingly valid reason for running away from life and remaining forever in the morally poisonous atmosphere of infancy.[56]

None of us is free of these moments of timidity and laziness. The real question is whether such an attitude prevails in the general conduct of our lives. Whenever, as in the case of fundamentalism's domination by fear, or the dependency we bring to our relationships, a refusal to grow up, that is, to individuate, dominates, then the hero task is forsworn.

Our resistance is understandable. We are finite, fearful, frail, and fragmented. Yet, and always yet, the way forward is the way through. Stephen Hoeller reports the ambivalence of a patient of Jung's who dreamt that she was in a pit from which she wished to escape, but she was also there with Jung who was pulling on her and saying, "Not out but through."[57] Later, whenever Jung would recount that dream, he said that the dreamer's unconscious had got it right: the way through a depression is *through* it and not out of it. Going through it will reveal its meaning, and unfold what the secret will of the Self may be.

Avoidance of this openness to going down and through will keep one in a form of spiritual adolescence, not unlike those whose spirituality is always "up there," safe from any real engagement with life. The bouncy spirituality of the so-called New Age movement and many fundamentalist groups is not only a flight from reality, with its necessary and autonomous visitations to the swamplands of the soul, but a shunning of the hero task as well. There are monsters, there are dragons, there are dangerous depths, and they are within us all the time. They are what give us our *gravitas* and our great capacity for enlargement through holding the tension between opposites.

---

[56] Ibid., par. 461.
[57] *The Gnostic Jung,* p. 197.

Another way in which the hero task may play out in the conduct of our lives, as well as that of a civilization, is found in our
capacity to sublimate the instinctual energies in service to an
abstract goal. The desire for comfort, the desire for safety, the
desire for nourishment—all represent legitimate human needs,
and yet when their agenda prevails, no civilization advances.
Nostalgia, which means, from its Greek roots, "pain for home,"
and *lethargy*, related to Lethe, the river of forgetfulness in the
underworld, and *sentimentality*, which takes a fine tuning of human perception and relatedness, sentiment, and drowns in it—all
suggest the difficulty of leaving home and standing on our own.

Earlier cultures understood the power of these regressive urges
and devised elaborate and extended rites of passage to evolve a
person out of dependency into an enlarged state of adulthood.
Sublimation is a transformation of those energies into individual
or cultural goals. The transformation of libido into higher forms
is the developmental agenda of every individual and every culture. It is also a religious value as it seeks to link the individual to
the symbolic task of engaging the mystery of life.

Fasting is an example of willed sacrifice of normal instinctual
demands in service to a higher value, such as the spiritual life or,
equally, to achieve an identification with the suffering of others.
So is celibacy when not driven by mere avoidance of what may
be difficult in life. The sacrifice of so many savior gods in ancient mythology is another form of sublimation of instinctual
life in service to such values as the transcendence of death, or
the redemption of a community through scapegoating or projective identification. As Jung noted, such sacrifice

> is the very reverse of regression—it is a successful canalization of
> libido into the symbolic equivalent of the mother, and hence a spiri-
> tualization of it. [58]

---

[58] *Symbols of Transformation*, CW 5, par. 398.

The "spiritualization" of the mother means that the energy which would drown in history and home is transformed into the building of new history and new home, both of which must in time be left also, if life is to be served.

We can see that the personal hero task, the task of becoming whomever the gods intended, not what the ego desires, benefits the culture ultimately through providing it with more differentiated values, more unique contributions to the collective.

This is the opposite to a narcissistic agenda, because it serves transcendent values embodied by the gods.

To not undertake our personal mission, then, is not only a failure of our own journey, but a failure for our culture. We live so much of our lives backward, not only dominated by history, but through backing our way nervously into the future. Little do we know that the future is waiting expectantly for us to become what we are destined to become when we have the courage to align our conscious choices with our individuation agenda.

What blocks us always is fear. In one of his most important utterances, Jung spares us not:

> The spirit of evil is fear, negation, the adversary who opposes life in its struggles for eternal duration and thwarts every great deed, who infuses into the body the poison of weakness and age through the treacherous bite of the serpent; he is the spirit of regression, who threatens us with bondage to the mother and with dissolution and extinction in the unconscious. For the hero, fear is a challenge and a task, because only boldness can deliver from fear. And if the risk is not taken, the meaning of life is somehow violated, and the whole future is condemned to hopeless staleness, to a drab grey lit only by will-o'-the-wisps.[59]

We can see, then, that the hero task is the act of life risking itself, life as verb, life *live-ing* as it were. But the serpent haunts

---

[59] Ibid., par. 551.

all our gardens, every day, whispering what we most want to hear—that the road is easy, that one can start tomorrow, that someone else will do it for us, that it is all a delusion anyhow, that nothing really matters in the end. On most days, the serpent's agenda is served. From time to time, however, we step out of the way to let life become through us. Thus, the hero task is less personal achievement, though it is that, than a service to the gods.

While bivouacked on the Danube, defending his people from the barbarian hoards, Marcus Aurelius wrote these lines to himself.

> At first day's light have in readiness, against disinclination to leave your bed, the thought that, "I am rising for the work of man." Must I grumble at setting out to do what I was born for, and for the sake of which I have been brought into the world? Is this the purpose of my creation, to lie here under the blankets and keep myself warm?
>
> . . . You have no real love for yourself; if you had, you would love your nature, and your nature's will. Craftsmen who love their trade will spend themselves to the utmost in laboring at it, even going unwashed and unfed, but apparently you hold your nature in less regard. . . . Is the service of the community of less worth in your eyes, and does it merit less devotion?[60]

That ancient emperor knew his task was to rise each dawn and fling himself against fear and torpor. To write of one's perilous and often harsh life as he did, with such equanimity and resolve, is to model the hero task, a task which challenges each of us at each day's humble dawn.

---

[60] *Meditations,* V, I, p. 77.

6
Descent/Ascent—Death/Rebirth

When I would recreate myself, I seek the darkest
wood, the thickest and most interminable and,
to the citizen, most dismal swamp. I enter a swamp
as a sacred place, a *sanctum sanctorum*. There is
the strength, the marrow, of Nature.
—Henry David Thoreau, "Walking."

Catabasis

The ancient stories are replete with descents, the catabasis to the underworld: Orpheus, Odysseus, Jesus, Aeneas, Dante, and many more. What is to be found down there? Certainly darkness, often monsters, sometimes treasures, and always something useful. We recall from the last chapter Jung's advice in the dream when the dreamer was in a deep hole: "Not out but through." Indeed, Dante does not come out; he goes through and reaches into the other side which leads him to the *Purgatorio* and finally the *Paradisio*.

What is this darkness down there, this tenebrous metaphor? It can swallow the ego for sure, and that is why we fear it so. But the darkness is also the *camera obscura* from whence new images will arise. The future will be carried by those images, even though at present they remain remote to the ego. The ego can drown, as it does in psychosis. Jung said to James and Nora Joyce when they brought their schizophrenic daughter to him for referral, "Your daughter is drowning in that sea in which you learned to swim."

Similarly, the darkness can reach up, if we stretch the metaphor, and seize the ego and occupy it, as sometimes occurs when the most somber of moods takes us hostage. The darkness down there is also the darkness of the womb, from which springs new life as well as the darkness of the tomb. Our fear of such nether places is projected onto spiders, serpents, mice, bats and other denizens of the dark. Yet all life begins in darkness, the warm, wet, frangible fertility of little things which become big things in time. In the suck and muck of slime the future will be formed and flung forth.

Just before her sixtieth birthday, a woman dreamt:

> Five girlfriends came down the hill, skipping and singing. It was a joyous, playful, frolicking time in the sun. We proceeded together on a walking excursion and came to a small cliff that dropped straight down. There was a narrow ledge on the other side.
>
> I said, "I'll go first."
>
> We began walking on the ledge, which sloped downward. I moved ahead and at the bottom of the incline found a dark lake with five women standing in it. All was dark. The women were submerged in the black water up to their necks. They wore close fitting black hoods that covered their hair and only their white painted faces showed.
>
> I looked down at my shoes on the dark ledge. They were "light," numinous, and their warmth was beginning to melt the hard packed ground and turn it green.
>
> I called to my friends coming behind me. "We need to get out. We will mess this up for them. We are melting it."

The dreamer had begun analysis in the context of a professional trauma. She had acted according to her best lights and been betrayed and humiliated to the degree that she had had to leave her employment. The mistreatment felt as a betrayal of her contract with the world: if she acted with kindness and good intentions, the world would reciprocate. At the same time, she was beginning to question some of her long-held religious beliefs, her life-long role as servant to others, and her relationship to her own journey. When she spoke of personal matters, she reflexively raised her hand to her mouth or her throat as though to hide her speech or suppress her voice. This dream was numinous to her, a little frightening, certainly fascinating; it commanded her attention over the next months of her analytic process.

What are we to make of this dream and these images? A dream can never be fully or finally interpreted. But a symbol is nature's best way of incarnating what cannot be otherwise expressed. Thus, its "explanation" will always be limited to some degree. (The dream is a phenomenon of nature; the work of the interpretative mind can at best only be an epiphenomenon). What is most important is how it becomes a felt experience for the dreamer. In this case the dreamer felt the dream to be very important to her, and she returned to it in many subsequent sessions without our ever understanding it in a completely satisfying way. Nonetheless, what we can see is that it is a dream of descent into the pool of the psyche.

The dreamer was particularly struck by the five mystery women in the pool, by their monkish attire, and by the transformation of her shoes into light that melted the earth into a luminous green. Her associations with the women was that it had to do with something deeply resonant within her, her instincts, her five senses, her sexuality, her archaic, powerful femininity. She intuited that these women were of an archetypal order that antedated all her belief systems. She also believed that her proximity to these women had transferred some sort of power to her which helped melt matters, and that her ground or standpoint had gained a luminosity. We cannot explain these elusive images, but we can feel our way into their meaning by association and intuition.

The dreamer was connecting to something that lay deeper than her beliefs, and deeper than her prior sense of self. At the same time, she felt an ambivalence toward the dream and the dream figures. They were a bit scary to her. Interestingly, their attire visually separated the head from the body, as her unconscious, protective gestures had also done.

In the course of our cultural conditioning, including the religious dogmas which may either sustain or contain the psyche's movements, we come to live most of the time out of the top half of our being. We live essentially as if we were machines with computer chips that define who we are, what the limits are, what is acceptable, and how we may interact with the world.

Not only is the psychic circumference of the family of origin a limiting factor, given its restricted purview of possibility, but so, for this dreamer, was her religious background, which defined what was acceptable and what was accessible. After a lifetime in religious life, she came to believe that her analysis had given her more religious experience and expression than the formal institution ever had.

Looking at those five women in the dream, seemingly rising from the depths, we sense the telluric origins not only of the body but also of the soul. We can feel that they constitute a religion older than religions, a spirituality so deeply grounded as to be timeless, or at least to provide access to the timeless. We also see that the dreamer has a power which she had never experienced consciously, a chthonic connection, a luminous force that melts what is frozen and gives her a standpoint in nature. The nature gods are much older than the gods of the head; the gods of the loins more ancient than the gods of the heart; the gods of earth and sea more ancient than gods of the skies.

Precisely because of this archaic power, this arcane mystery, the dreamer was ambivalent toward the descent. She felt as if she had perhaps stumbled on the mysteries—not unlike Actaeon coming upon Artemis bathing—and would have to pay for the transgression. "We need to get out," she tells her intrapsychic companions. And yet the image of the women rising from the depths continued to haunt her. She returned to the dream repeatedly and at this writing is still working on it. Meanwhile, what her analyst has seen and is seeing is a deepening of the person, a more confident person, increasingly grounded in her own reality, and able to speak from that place.

If the energy shows up in a dream image, then it already exists in the psyche of the dreamer. The invisible has been rendered visible. The task of consciousness is to begin to consider this energy, to weigh its presence and to incorporate it into the conduct of daily life. The dream has brought gifts which are continuing to this moment. Before one can deepen as a person, one must visit the deeps within. We cannot ascend without first descending.

Jung reported a now well-known dream of entering a subterranean cavern and encountering a huge, phallic-shaped object and hearing his mother's voice which said, "That is the man-eater!"[61] This numinous, ithyphallic presence haunted his early years, both with fear and with shame, even though the etymology of the word *phallus* means "bright, or shining," which is also an etymological root for the word *god*. After this numinous, intimidating yet compelling dream, all the talk about Lord Jesus from his parson father and his many parson uncles seemed unreal, ethereal, or at least incomplete without the complement of the underground god.

Strangely, in the dark underground, the chthonic god was "shining." Is it not interesting that our ancestors recognized the brilliance, the numinosity of what the phallus represented, before it was driven underground? Only in later decades could Jung revisit that dream, tell it to others, and recognize its compensatory value not only in his own life, but to the one-sided, timorous, ethereal theology of his childhood environment. The psyche had told him that just as there are upper mysteries, there are

---

[61] *Memories, Dreams, Reflections*, pp. 12f.

lower mysteries as well, and one cannot be excluded without great cost to the other.

In time Jung came to regard his father's religious attitudes as defenses against the reality of experience, as splitting off those telluric powers which also govern the universe. If one worships the god on high exclusively, as his father did, the god below will wreak its revenge, as it did by keeping his father in a life-long depression and spiritual paralysis. What is denied above will assert itself from below. This applies not only to our personal relationship to the unconscious, but to the enduring mysteries of the cosmos as well.

Jung also reports other dreams of descent. In one of these he digs below the earth to find the skeletons of pre-historic creatures, and in another he finds a giant radiolarian in a pool of water. He writes:

> [These dreams] aroused in me an intense desire for knowledge, so that I awoke with a beating heart. These two dreams decided me overwhelmingly in favor of science, and removed all my doubts.[62]

At first Jung wanted to become an archeologist, but as a child from a poor family he lacked the resources to pursue this passion; instead he accepted a scholarship to medical school, and in time became an archeologist of the soul. In his day the study of the soul was the exclusive preserve of clerics but, given the waning efficacy of institutional forms, there arose a new discipline, psychoanalysis, which lay somewhere between religion and science, taking its heuristic ground in the unexplored psyche.

Anabasis

The descent may of course end in stasis, in dissolution and defeat. The cycle demands an ascent, a going up in order to bring the gift into consciousness. Even those dreams or life experi-

---

[62] Ibid., p. 85.

ences which pull us under have gifts, although we may not recognize them at the time. We may even reject their message when they become conscious.

A nonbiologically based depression, for example, tells us that the ego's desire to invest libido in a certain direction has been autonomously nixed by the psyche. This experience, common to us all, is felt as a defeat, and the ego will struggle to reinstitute its intention. Yet, the psyche clearly has another agenda. This is a signal that we are investing libido in an exhausted place, that other parts of our psyche want attention.

One of the first signs of this descent is ennui, or boredom, perhaps even in the career for which one prepared so diligently. Yet, whether chosen rightly or wrongly at a certain stage of life, no single choice can engage one forever. When the intimations of the psyche are ignored over a long time, the psyche will withdraw even more libido and one will be pulled into the underground, as Jung's father was in his depression and Jung himself during his middle passage. And who has not, like Dante, found oneself, at some point, in a dark wood, having lost the way? If one pays no heed, takes no action to change priorities, the depression will persist.

The ascent requires not only the climb out of the depths, but also the necessary task of integrating what has been learned into consciousness. Orpheus returns, but doubts his rapprochement with the gods, turns back for confirmation and thereby his Eurydice is lost forever.

Jesus returns, Dante breaks through the limits of Hell by going down and through. The poet Saint-John Perse writes *Anabasis* in 1924 about an ancient conqueror of Asiatic wastes and about the arrival at the end of the journey where he finds,

> over and above the actions of men on the earth,
> many omens on the way, many seeds on the way,
> and under unleavened fine weather, in one

great breath of the earth, the whole feather
of harvest! . . .
I have seen the earth parceled out in vast spaces
and my thought is not heedless of the navigator.[63]

The "Navigator" is the soul, the gods, the compelling summons of individuation, which this ancient worthy humbly acknowledged.

We need to remember that what one has learned from nature,
from our encounter with the world or the psyche, may not be
pleasing to the ego. And yet, such knowledge always expands our
purview, and therefore our freedom. Much of what we have to
learn of ourselves, our shadow encounters, will prove disquieting
to our ego's fantasies. Much of what we learn of the world and
its deceits will undermine our idealism. Much of what we bring
back to the surface will actually make living more painful, but it
will be more honest.

A character in a Milan Kundera novel illustrates this bitter-
sweet learning of the world as she rises from the great grief of a
lost child to a re-engagement with the world as it is. Standing
before the grave of her child, she says to herself,

My darling, don't think I don't love you or that I didn't love you,
but it's precisely because I loved you that I couldn't have become
what I am today if you were still here. It is impossible to have a
child and despise the world as it is, because that's the world we've
put the child into. The child makes us care about the world, think
about its future, willingly join in its racket and its turmoils, take its
incurable stupidity seriously. By your death you deprived me of the
pleasure of being with you, but at the same time you set me free.
Free in my confrontation with a world I don't like. And the reason I
can allow myself to dislike it is that you're no longer here. My dark
thoughts can't bring any curse down on you. I want to tell you now,

---

[63] *Anabasis,* p. 37.

all these years after you left me, that I've come to understand your death as a gift and that I've finally accepted that dreadful gift.[64]

The *anabasis* up and out of the well of grief has brought to her a sobering animosity with the world as it is. Only the sentimental would insist on a happy ending for her. She has earned her knowledge, her release and it has been integrated into a freedom from the tentacles of the world which otherwise would bind her to hope for what is hopeless.

She is, as we all are, what Marcus Aurelius, citing the stoic Epictetus, identified as, "a poor soul burdened with a corpse."[65]

One man, the CEO of a company, dreamt that he had ascended to the peak of a mountain only to find that there was another mountain to be climbed. He asked himself whether he had the strength to climb that next mountain, and found himself answering, "no, nor do I want to." When we reflected on the dream he concluded that all his life he had been programmed to be ambitious, forever setting new goals. His mother was haunted by the thought of being a "nobody" and his father had failed to satisfy her unrequited social ambitions. He was their *Wunderkind*, and played the part to the hilt. His single mindedness brought him an impressive resumé, but gave him no respite. As a result he had burned through three marriages, moved from corporate niche to corporate niche, lived in virtually every major city in America and two abroad.

"I have never known peace, or acceptance, or a sense of real achievement in all these years," he lamented. His Faustian journey, undertaken with the best of intent, was, he concluded, living the life his parents had planned for him and that his culture reinforced. It was very difficult for him to imagine stepping down from that coursing stallion he had always ridden, or perhaps had

---

[64] *Identity*, p. 59.
[65] Aurelius, *Meditations*, IV, 41, p. 73.

ridden him. His ascent had removed him from life, not conquered it as he fantasized. For all his achievements, for all the summits, life felt empty to him now, even wasted. The end of his analysis coincided with his decision to leave corporate life, retire early, try to make peace with his scattered family, and to decide, perhaps for the first time in his life, what he wanted for himself. Ironically, the toughest mountain he ever had to conquer was the one he left behind.

This gentleman had to climb out of the Slough of Success before he could reach some peak of failure and through that journey recover his life. His descent had occurred through rational ascent, and his descent into the underworld of dreams led him to his saving ascent.

When one thinks of what is to be found at the end of the journey, at the pinnacle of wisdom, one thinks of Yeats's mature reflections on the nature of our journey, on the great griefs and the heart-sorrow which is our constant companion, and yet the possibility of finding the capacity to say "yes" to that life through what he called "tragic gaiety." Only months before he died, Yeats observes a lapis lazuli carving from Japan, then describes the scene of ancient sages sitting on a mountain top, observing the human tumult on the plains below. He confesses his

> Delight to imagine them seated there;
> There, on the mountain and the sky,
> On all the tragic scene they stare.
> One asks for mournful melodies;
> Accomplished fingers begin to play.
> Their eyes mid many wrinkles, their eyes,
> Their ancient, glittering eyes, are gay.[66]

To have gone to the mountain top, to have completed the ascent, one must finally discern whether one climbed the right

---

[66] "Lapis Lazuli," in M.L. Rosenthal, ed., *Selected Poems,* p. 160.

mountain. The testimony of observers does not count. Only the confirmation of our quite separate psyches will suffice. When one reaches such a pinnacle of clarity, one may then be able to look upon the world with the keen eye, and perhaps even the detachment, of the ancients.

7
The Gods

It must be troubling for the god who loves you
To ponder how much happier you'd be today
Had you been able to glimpse your many futures.
—Carl Dennis, "The God Who Loves You."

What is a god? At the semiotic level, the word "god" is the symbol we use to point toward that which is truly transcendent (or Wholly Other, as the Swiss theologian Karl Barth defined it), and essentially unknowable. Just as Immanuel Kant asserted two centuries ago that we can never know the *Ding-an-Sich,* the thing in itself, in the natural world, even less may we know the transcendent realm. Anything which the finite mind presents as a construct of the infinite reveals more of human imagination than of the infinite itself. To "speak theologically" is a virtual contradiction in terms, and yet we are driven to such an oxymoron, to seek understanding of that which is wholly other and transcends our limited condition.

Nonetheless, there may be clues as to the Other. Certainly such world religions as Judaism see clues in the sands of the Sinai and atop the mount of the Decalogue; Christianity, in the paradigm and preaching of the Nazarene sees hints; and Islam sees them in the witness of Mohammed. Each expression, however, is strained through the alembic of tribal sensibility and world-view of the ego in that time and that place.

Such "god-talk" utilizes language as an epiphenomenal construct to momentarily embody a primal event. The god is incarnated by consciousness through the image which arises out of such encounters. The image presented to consciousness is not the god, limited as it is to the inadequate tools of finite sensibility, yet such an image is filled with, and driven by, energy which derives from the god.

It is the familiar fall of consciousness to confuse the two—the image with the energy—and be bewitched by the image. The image is but the symbolic bridge between the energic source and the finite sensibility. However, the ego frequently literalizes the image, becomes enthralled and tips over into the oldest of religious sins, idolatry. As Kierkegaard reminds us, the god which can be named is not God;[67] as Paul Tillich reminds, God is the god which appears from out behind the image of the god which has disappeared.[68] In other words, the autonomy and wholly other character of divinity is forever protean, shape shifting, however much ego consciousness wishes to fix and fashion it.

This confusion between image and the energy which charges the image leads not only to idolatry, but intrapsychically occurs all the time, as when, for example, the ego privileges its own limited reality over the larger frame of the Self. One legend reports that the gods laughed themselves to death when one of them, a regional deity called Yahweh, proclaimed himself God.

So the ego forever seeks the posture of divinity, until times when the neglected Self imposes itself upon the ego in such fashion as to break its delusion of sovereignty. The ego thinks it is the Self, and the religious sensibility thinks the image is the god. So our history of delusion continues, in part because of the limits of ego capacity, and in part because of its hidden agenda of seeking control of what is wholly beyond its ken. Thus so much of theology and personal psychology manifest as psychopathology, a wounded expression of the soul's magnitude.

What can be said of the gods which has not been said? Who

---

[67] *Concluding Unscientific Postscript,* p. 142.
[68] *The Courage To Be,* p. 86.

are they? Why does a relatively rational person even refer to the gods today? What can we say, if anything, about them? Are they naught but our projections? Are they in fact the old parent figures in the sky which we inherited from tribal history, from when the heavens were "up there" somewhere? Are they watching us with some large book, some doomsday accounting, the purpose of which is to frighten us into right conduct? Or can a person who believes in the metaphysical reality of God A, his god, but not God B, his neighbor's god, still find a way to listen rationally to all this palaver?

Can the fearful even open to any of these questions about the gods, or are they too insecure in their belief to allow some slack for rumination? Why bother, even? Why not just celebrate this evanescent moment between two great darknesses, before passing into oblivion? And does anyone—in a culture awash in material abundance, and, frankly, too jaded to give a damn—even worry about these questions anymore?

Just this morning I received the following dream from a forty-year-old businessman who has been struggling with his faith, with his career, with the disparate parts of his life.

> I am holding a box about three feet by three feet, juggling it above my head. It's almost empty, but a small crab falls out. There is a woman there. She desires this box.
>
> I am at a meeting. I am under the table. I touch the shoe of a man, playfully. He is aggravated with me. I am playful because I don't feel anything is at stake at the meeting.
>
> I am struggling with an elk with big horns. His antlers are velvety, and on them is written a word which I think is "covenant," or "obligation." This is God, I am wrestling with, I think. The elk is trying to get his way. I am not sure who will win. I haven't given up the struggle. Who will win?

As in all dreams, the dreamer's personal associations are critical. He feels that the box is "numinous," though why is not clear. The box is empty yet dynamic, and his physical posture in struggling to hold it up is identical to his position in grappling with the horns of the elk. He also associates the box with the Arc of the Covenant, which is not only an historic reference, but an image of the dilemma through which he was currently suffering, an issue of commitment, specifically to his faith and to his relationships. The woman present is nondescript, but she desires the box and whatever it contains. His association with the crab was something which had to do with sexuality, which, like the elemental crustacean, was his "fly in the ointment." He further associated the crab with something playful, like a sand crab which skitters across the beach, precisely at the margin where sea meets land.

Regarding the second part of the dream, he noted that the night before he had attended another tiresome meeting of his church board in which matters of building code enforcement had preoccupied the group, as well as their voting down a service to the needy which he felt his church should have provided. He believed he was under the table, not only because of his many theological doubts, which he had to keep from his congregation to remain a member, but the feeling that much of what occupied their attention was trivial.

In the third part of the dream, he said he simply "knew" that the elk, which he considered a magnificent creature, to be God incarnated. (This dreamer has a strong interest in nature and believes he finds God more in nature than in theology.) He believed that his struggle with the elk-god was an expression of his life dilemma, namely, "How can I keep my integrity in a world of banality, sexuality and the numinous"? He also wondered, "How can I continue to live my life in a faithful way and yet acknowledge self-interest?"

Like the antlers of the elk, the dreamer is "on the horns" of several dilemmas. He is considering a change of career, he is shuttling back and forth between responsibilities to both professions; he is in a marriage which has its pluses and minuses, and yet he wishes to remain faithful to all his commitments. He is torn between his covenant with God, and with his wife, and his own desires and individuation needs, and he wants to be faithful to both ends of these dilemmas.

The crab that falls from the numinous box is a part of his nature, and a part of his divinity, although it remains highly problematic to live out. He feels that the woman in the dream is a kind of anima figure, transcendent to his ego state, and that she is, "intuitive, accepting, nonjudgmental." Thus, he feels that she is a part of himself which speaks from the soul, while his ego speaks from the culture from which he has come and whose values he still affirms.

A significant aspect of his dilemma of choice between duty and desire is that he never felt playful in the face of duty. Hence the crab suggests both instinctual sexuality and playfulness at the same time, both of which the heart desires and the ego constricts. On the one hand, he wants to maintain support of respected values, and on the other hand, he seeks the *joie de vivre* which makes life rich. The crab, lowly creature as it is, is an image of divinity, for, like Hermes, it goes back and forth between the two worlds of surf and sand, unconscious and ego.

The lowly crab carries the ambivalent values of all creation, not unlike the dung beetle or scarab of Egyptian myth. The scarab rose from dead matter, the refuse of life, and brought new life. So, too, to this dreamer, the lowliest of creatures carries the highest of values. This is a theological value, and a psychological value of archetypal character. The rejected stone becomes the cornerstone of the new structure, the lowliest shall sit at the throne, and the meek shall inherit the earth.

In the second part of the dream, he made a quick connection between the dream actor's playfulness and the banality of the previous night's meeting, but he also acknowledged not only that his being under the table spoke to the need to keep his shadow life hidden, but that his position there was actually an inferior role which he felt his career had called him to play. His position before the church community was that of abasement rather than the humility of the servant. He also felt that the image was suggesting that "you don't belong here."

For this dreamer, the mighty elk was a fit carrier of the divine. Moreover, its antlers were velvety, suggestive of the transition that the Godhead was undergoing in his understanding. The molting antlers were like outdated beliefs he had left behind, and yet had to hide from his far more conservative colleagues. He had no problem seeing God in nature, and certainly considered the elk a spiritual presence. His struggle with the elk was symbolic of his struggle to live according to his conscious beliefs and yet honor his own nature. At dream's end, the outcome of the struggle is clearly up for grabs.

I immediately thought of Yeats's poem about the struggle with divinity:

> Now his wars on God begin;
> At stroke of midnight God shall win.[69]

And also of that great struggle which beset the Jesuit priest Gerard Manley Hopkins who, in one of the so-called "Terrible Sonnets," because they are so full of theological terror, struggles with a beast that threatens to devour him, who "lays a lionlimb against" him, who comes at him with "darksome devouring eyes," who terrifies him, and whom at last he recognizes in astonishment: "I wretch lay wrestling with (my God!) my God."[70]

Gustave Flaubert, in "A Simple Heart," recounts the story of a simple servant prized by all for her faithful service while she is

---

[69] "The Four Ages of Man," in Rosenthal, ed., *Selected Poems,* p. 157.
[70] "Carrion Comfort," in *The Norton Anthology of Poetry*, p. 858.

laughed at behind her back for her naiveté. She, like the dreamer, connects with nature, and has only loved one thing in her life, which is her parrot. She has an epiphanic vision of the parrot and knows she has seen God. She is laughed at for this amusing blasphemy, but Flaubert leaves no doubt that this simple heart has touched more divinity than all the sophisticates of Paris.[71]

Dietrich Bonhoeffer also wrestled with both his personal and his theological dilemma in Flensburg concentration camp before his execution by the Nazis. Did God create this place, he wondered? He concluded that his task was to find his way through to the will of God for him in that terrible place, that place where every act of every day was an ethical nightmare.[72]

How similar is the struggle of Bonhoeffer to this dreamer's: "How can I keep my integrity in a such a world as I find myself?" The dream is a fit expression of that dilemma, and in its way a profound expression of the appearance of divinity as the third which embodies the terrible tension of the two, the tension of the opposites. How is this person to resolve the tension between his commitment to his ethical vows and the autonomous demands of his nature which desire a more honest religiosity, and a more ardent sexual life? No one would choose such a dilemma, but something inside chooses for us and places us at the crossroads where only crucifixion of the ego can occur.

We can neither predict how this will turn out, nor can we advise what is right for another's soul. (The opinion of the analyst is usually irrelevant in the adjudication of questions which the soul proposes.) As Jung has repeatedly argued, the tension of opposites must be held until its meaning, the unknown "third," appears. The unknown third is in effect the emergence of the meaning of this question in the developmental process of the

---

[71] "A Simple Heart," in *Three Tales.*
[72] See Bonhoeffer, *Letters and Papers from Prison.*

individual. In one person's life, fidelity to a particular vow is something which must be honored, suffered through, to a meaningful sacrifice; for another, the vow, however honestly sworn, is a fixation which arrests the development of the person.

Either path offers a slippery slope of rationalizations; either path is a choice with painful consequences. How interesting it is, then, that the "third" which appears in this dreamer's psyche is God, assuming the form which the dreamer cherishes, the dream of a wild god, commanding respect, a god with whom one wrestles toward an uncertain outcome. How often the gods appear to us that way, full of mystery, full of riddles, full of paradoxes that crack the brain and divide the heart. But those are the gods for you, and that is why they are gods.

So, who then are these gods, and why do we call them *gods?* Calling them gods is itself a metaphor which designates the respect we have for the mystery, the autonomy, the ineluctable energy they embody. The gods arise out of our encounter with depth, with mystery. There are as are many gods as there are such encounters. For those who once lived in an animistic universe, a world now judged superstitious, primitive, the world was resonant with divinity. Recall Gerard Manley Hopkins: "The world is *charged* with the grandeur of God."[73]

The subsequent historical development of ego moved to the "theological epoch" where the powers of the universe were personified by specific gods. The next era was the "mechanistic" epoch where science and education were utilized to identify and master the secrets of another metaphor, that of the great interlocking mechanism.

As these epochs progress, there is an increasing mastery over matter, even to the point of projecting the fantasy of transcending death, but always with a concomitant loss of the numi-

---

[73] See above, p. 21, note 15.

nous. The banishment of the gods leads ultimately to a dreary, mechanistic universe. When the word spread throughout the ancient world that the great nature god Pan was dead, there was no rejoicing. He was replaced by the stern monotheistic gods of the Judeo-Christian-Islamic world, who were in turn replaced by the modern reigning deities of Positivism, Materialism, Hedonism, and most of all, the great god Progress. And so the world gets emptier and emptier, and the clients pile up in therapists' offices, huddle fearfully in houses of ancestral worship, or numb out through television, drugs or even an obsessive preoccupation with health. The gods have hardly gone; they have simply gone underground, and they constantly resurface in the form of our various pathologies.

What I believe to be the most important observation about "modernism" (a designated phase of history whose central project was the dismantlement of the metaphysical apparatus necessary for the theological epoch, and its replacement by such dead ends as structuralism, nihilism and deconstructionism), is the paragraph written by Jung over six decades ago.

> We think we can congratulate ourselves on having already reached such a pinnacle of clarity, imagining that we have left all these phantasmal gods far behind. But what we have left behind are only verbal spectres, not the psychic facts that were responsible for the birth of the gods. We are still as much possessed by autonomous psychic contents as if they were Olympians. Today they are called phobias, obsessions, and so forth; in a word, neurotic symptoms. The gods have become diseases; Zeus no longer rules Olympus but rather the solar plexus, and produces curious specimens for the doctor's consulting room, or disorders the brains of politicians and journalists who unwittingly let loose psychic epidemics on the world.[74]

---

[74] "Commentary on 'The Secret of the Golden Flower,' " *Alchemical Studies,* CW 13, par. 54.

Each epoch finds its own form of hubris, of course, but ours is especially enchanted by the delusion of "progress." As has popularly been observed, myths are other people's gods. "Ours" of course are "real." So, what has disappeared? Zeus? Has not the power that name once embodied simply been transferred into the power of Progress? Has not the power complex become a disorder of our history, our institutions, and sometimes our private lives? What disappeared—the name, the verbal husk—but that energy which rightly is perceived as divinity has slipped into the underground. Yes, Pan was slain, slain by solemn sobriety, yet, imprisoned underground, still attacks individuals in panic attacks and collectively in the excesses of our popular culture and our nationalistic frenzies.

Yes, the verbal specter of Aphrodite has disappeared, but what she embodied as an energy worthy of devotion is today reincarnated as mood disorders and relational sterility. Gods ignored, which is to say, primal energies repressed, split off, projected, today show up as neuroses. They are the animating wounds manifest in history, acted out in families, public forums or the sundry deformations of the private soul.

Admittedly, to refer to such phenomena as gods is an astonishing hyperbole to the healing community and a blasphemy to the circle of believers. To the former, who have banished the depths, who have split *psyche* off from psychology and psychiatry, such a metaphor as the gods is only a metaphoric excess. Yet they themselves have unconsciously deified pharmacology, the *DSM IV*, and so-called "treatment plans." What they ignore is the meaning of the wound, the task of the suffering, and the spirit's agenda for the healing.

For the true believers, or those lazy in rigor, such use of the gods seems blasphemous because it is seemingly someone else's tribal god, and not theirs. Yet, they have violated the first commandment: to set no other gods before God. The god they worship is the tribal god, not the god who destroys itself upon reification and goes underground in search of another form. They commit the oldest of religious sins, idolatry, by worshipping the image of god they have made.

Looked at archetypally, a god is the image which arises out of a depth experience, an encounter with mystery. For this reason, divinity is always renewing itself. How could it possibly be fixed? It is energy, not image. The image is only the transient husk of divinity. Divinity floods the husk, renders it numinous, and when the human ego seeks to fix it, worship it and constrict it in service to its own ego security agenda, the god "dies," which is to say, leaves the husk to reincarnate elsewhere. This is the meaning of the "death of god" motif, which may be found in the ancient mythologies of all peoples, long before Nietzsche's mid-nineteenth-century pronouncement.

Such acknowledgements of the death of god is, on the one hand, a simple observation of how a particular image has grown so reified, so constricted as to no longer move the heart and spirit of the people. As a child I was confused that so much of the rhetoric about god was creative, joyful and transformative, and scary too, yet so little of the effects upon the lives of those around me bore the mark of such energy. While lacking the capacity to comprehend at the time, I was experiencing the discrepancy between the rhetoric which moves the brain, and the *de facto*, dissociative manifestations of the soul's diminishment found in depression, infantilization, intimidation, stultification and a covert effort to legitimize the social and moral status quo. Later I came to understand these qualities served the security needs of the ego, and never acknowledged the presence of the gods in our midst.

And, on the other hand, such affirmations as the death of god are a paradoxical way of affirming and acceding to the freedom, the autonomy upon which the gods insist. The more we seek to define them, constrict them, the further they slip from us. This is why the pronouncements of the televangelists ring so hollow. Their frenzied certainty is a confession of uncertainty, and their insistence is evidence of the existential insecurity they are trying to treat. They tip their theological hands as quickly as they take checks from the frightened.

Why should one not be insecure in the presence of great mystery? Who says that it is preferable to serve our frangible egos rather than the gods? Is faith, by definition, not based on uncertainty rather than certainty? Is not uncertainty, and a humbling recognition of the autonomy of the gods, what actually characterizes a truly religious attitude?

Of course the phrase "the death of god" is confusing because it feeds our temptation to erect metaphysical structures. The word is thought to refer to the thing; the concept to its content; the image to contain the energy which created it. This natural tendency in us all leads to profound misunderstanding. Even much of analytic psychology has been misunderstood because of thinking that metaphors like *anima* and *shadow* and *Self* might be concrete.

Jungians frequently capitalize Self not to reify but to distinguish it from the ego-self. The Self is a verb; the psyche *selves*. The Self is not seen, but its activities are experienced in all aspects of our being from our biochemical processes to our dreams. The Self is not god; to assume so would be to fall into the familiar trap. No, the Self is a metaphor for that kind of energy in which the activity of divinity may be witnessed. So, too, the burning bush of the Hebrew scriptures is not god; it is the husk aflame with the energy of divinity. To worship a bush is to slay the god through literalism. Though understandable, literalism is blasphemous, impious, idolatrous, and, finally, irrelevant.

When a person has a religious experience, he or she is possessed by an energy from an unknown source. That source could be the gods, or some intrapsychic complex. Who among us has not been possessed, as least for awhile, by a powerful belief, a moment of insecurity which converts to a paranoid thought or an obsessive-compulsive defense ritual, or even a long-term psychotic disorder such as bigotry? Since these events are intrapsychic, they are by definition real for us and we tend to lack the discretionary powers to evaluate them objectively. How many religions, cults, fashionable movements have arisen from a momentary possession of a charismatic individual or from tribal *representations collectives*? Jung makes an important distinction:

> It is not a matter of indifference whether one calls something a "mania" or a "god." To serve a mania is detestable and undignified, but to serve a god is full of meaning and promise because it is an act of submission to a higher, invisible, and spiritual being. The personification enables us to see the relative reality of the autonomous system, and not only makes its assimilation possible but also depotentiates the daemonic forces of life. When this god is not acknowledged, egomania develops, and out of this mania comes sickness.[75]

To the modern mind, the acknowledgement of a god in the midst of a "possession," or what we might call an enthusiasm (from *en-theos,* the god within), a compulsion, an addiction, an anxiety state, seems antiquated at best and superstitious at worst. But Jung's point is profound. Our ancestors came to recognize that something took them over, some energy that was autonomous and compelling. To remember the god who may be at work, who may be offended, is to begin to relocate the ego in a humble yet consciously responsible relationship to that energy. To speak of the god who possesses me is already to be in partnership with that god, that energy, and to begin to recognize what steps are necessary to recover a right relationship to it. Today we may use more neutral language such as anger manage-

---

[75] Ibid., par. 55.

ment rather than possession by Ares, but either way we need to come to an accounting with that energy which operates at will within us.

I live in a city where a woman recently drowned her five children. She operated under delusions of personal guilt and inadequacy, greatly fostered by her fundamentalist friends. She believed she could free her children from herself and speed them to a better world. The older ones fought to breathe when she forced their heads under the water. While she had been under psychiatric and pharmacological care, neither had possessed the power to reduce the urgency of her mania. At the time of the five murders she was not in treatment or taking her medicine, but she did have regular doses of fundamentalism.

How could Medea still live among us, we ask? But what parent has not nursed homicidal thoughts even while simultaneously adoring their children. In the real world of the psyche, ambivalent thoughts exist side by side, although consciousness will privilege one over the other. But where does the other, the rejected thought, then go? It will perforce find a way to express itself in some other, perhaps terrible, venue.

Let us acknowledge that next to Hera within us is also Ares, and that for every faithful Antigone there is also a murderous Medea. For those who have recognized these presences, one can only walk in humility and supplication before the gods which drive us. When modern psychology thinks beyond, or through, a neurosis (and what kind of fantasy of the "nerves" is that?), and metaphorically thinks rather of a wounded or neglected god, then we restore the mystery, and the depth dimension, to human experience.

We are bewitched by language all the time. We *have* cancer as a foreign element rather than say we *are* cancer, that it is part of how we are living. We have a complex rather than saying the complex is part of our intrapsychic reality. Naturally the ego seeks to protect itself by distancing, but it is thereby all the more in a state of virtual dissociation. The modern will hardly grasp the value of identifying the god at work within, but the point remains: to what degree are we in relationship to the invisible world, and to what degree is it operating autonomously and either aiding or victimizing us?

Archetypal scholar Ginette Paris puts the dilemma this way:

> What the ancient Greeks called an insult to a divinity brought upon mortals divine wrath, a tragic spell. As in neurosis and psychosis, this sort of suffering led nowhere and produced nothing. An ancient Greek whose destiny was going badly would ask which divinity he or she had offended. This questioning was part of what we would call therapy.[76]

On the one hand this poor woman who drowned her children had the devils inside her head, and the devils outside denouncing her sins. The therapeutic task is to acknowledge the power of an idea, especially one repulsive to the ego, and to honor its power lest one fall prey to its autonomous enactment. By proclaiming such thoughts evil and repressing them, we can only breed monsters in the unconscious. This is the fallacy of fundamentalism: the fantasy that one can rid oneself of bad thoughts and then perform only right conduct. If this were true we would have conscious abundance rather than constricted souls, joyous paganism rather than joyless orthodoxy, and less effort to control the erotic insurrection of the prophet who came to them promising more abundant life.

But, one argues, this contemporary Medea was in touch with the gods, at least the god presented by her cohorts, a god of judgment and punitive character. And how much good did that god do her children? The problem here, of course, is that not only was she surrounded by frightened contemporaries who pro-

---

[76] *Pagan Meditations,* p. 101.

jected their fear into a negative father complex as a deity, but that her own ego powers were impaired, in part by culture, and in part by biology.

The corrective or compensatory powers of therapy and pharmacology were interrupted and could no longer provide her any balancing with the forces of fearful consensus and errant chemistry. Had those powers been in place, her consciousness reinforced, she might have been able to sort through the maelstrom of conflicting emotion to reach moments of personal clarity and resolve. Her children might still be alive. But we will never know that, although we do know currently that in prison, with treatment, she has reportedly regained her sanity and has now to live with the full enormity of her acts. So, the hidden god here is the great god Fear, a god who holds sway over many a soul. Who cannot identify this god will end by being governed by it unconsciously. As Jung said, to serve a mania is detestable; to serve a god is meaningful.

To personify the god is to acknowledge that it is not only powerful but that one can come into some sort of conscious relationship to it. The god Fear, unacknowledged, becomes a tyrannical murderer. To personify the god brings the possibility of assimilating the contents into consciousness and thereby removing their demonic power. When a person is in the grips of the demonic, and the crowd reinforces that energy, the ordinary individual has little purchase on consciousness.

This diminishment of consciousness, this *abaissement de niveau mentale*, not only happens to the Medeas among us, but to all of us in the psychopathology of everyday life. In our time, we are obliged to acknowledge as our moral benchmark the searing memory of how an entire nation can be seized by a mania, can overthrow its achievements in the arts, sciences and humanities, can give its soul to a demonic orator, a charismatic figure who speaks to the fear within each, who seduces a nation into raising their arm in salute to the one who will save them from themselves, and yet ends by bringing fire down upon their heads.

Even the fantasy of a thousand-year Reich is a symptom of a fearful resistance to change and ambiguity and remains an unwitting confession of the fears of insufficiency, of inferiority and its compensatory rhetoric of domination and superiority through projective identification with the hero archetype. Should we be surprised when we recall the archetypal foundation of the marriage of such animosity and such ardor, such hope for *Vereinigung*, or unity, at the expense of the values which are suppressed to make it possible? The miraculous mating of Ares and Aphrodite produced three offspring. One was Harmony, the reconciliation of opposites. But the other two were *Phobos* (Fear) and *Deimos* (Terror). In our time, this mating of animosity and ardor produced *Schrecklichkeit*, or Terror, as national policy.

So, who says the gods have gone? They have simply departed the old husks and have moved invisibly into new loci. Yet, as we are reminded by the Hymn to Demeter, "Difficult are the gods for men to see."[77] In another time, in the animistic, and even in the theological epochs, one could see the gods at work in the moment's fantasy, in the apocalyptic event of history, in the longed-for appearance of a sail upon the wine-dark sea, in the ascent of the rosy-fingered dawn, and in the telluric powers which bring us all to ground.

Such illuminations sometimes pleased, sometimes uplifted, sometimes terrified, but always moved the recipients. They sought to preserve these moments of numinous engagement through the development of cultural forms, specifically: a) dogma, what happened and what did it mean; b) ritual, how can we recreate the experience; and c) cultic observances, what difference does it make to our tribe?

---

[77] Cited by Calasso, *Literature and the Gods,* p. 5.

Each of these cultural forms seeks to retain a vital connection to the primal experience, to recreate the wonder and terror of first things. But the passage of time takes one further and further from the initial wonder or terror. As a result, the ego tends to seek its former level of satisfaction and reiterates with greater urgency. So, even as one urgently, even frantically, seeks to maintain the divine aura of dogma, rigidify the ritual, and convert cultic experience to cult security, the gods slip away and grow invisible again. At those moments a person, a tribe, a civilization experiences a profound crisis of identity, meaning and direction. Such a dilemma is the story of our time.

We are not absent the gods; quite the contrary. We have too many of them, too many surrogates with which the ego seeks to resist the spiritual vacuum of modernism. Besieged by pseudo-deities such as Power, Wealth, Health, Pleasure, Progress, we grow more and more alienated from nature, from each other, and from ourselves. This is why depth psychology had to be invented at the end of the nineteenth century. Too much human life fell into the gap between institutional religion on the one hand and institutional medicine on the other. To ask, "What god is at work here, what god forgotten, offended, split off, projected," is to undertake the healing task of therapy. And yet this sort of metaphoric formulation is ridiculed by most representatives of the modern therapeutic community.

Only depth psychologists dare use such language. This is why the therapeutic focus has fallen on behaviors, which can be observed, rather than the invisible gods which cannot; why cognitions are restructured rather than engaging the force which gives them sovereignty in our souls; why pharmacology is deified when so much humanity lies beyond the sum of biochemistry. To use such metaphoric, archetypally based language today is to immediately be marginalized if not ridiculed. But that is why we have confused cure with healing, treatment modalities with meaning, and the finite agenda of the ego with the infinite agencies of the soul.

The loss of relationship to the invisible powers makes the visible powers all the more powerful. We have corporate moguls running government, as deceitfully as they ran corporations, not the philosopher-kings that Plato suggested, or even the merely powerful as Machiavelli described. Woe befalls those who live only in the world of the concrete, for it will fail them, as it already has. As Roberto Callaso observes,

> "Where there are no gods, the phantoms reign," Novalis had prophesied. Now one could go a step further and say: gods and phantoms will alternate on the scene with equal rights. There is no longer a theological power capable of taking charge and putting them in order. In which case, who will risk dealing with them, arranging them?[78]

Thus the spectacle of modern social and political interaction is little more than the exercise of the old will to power serving contemporary neuroses. The outcome is no longer in doubt. We end in neuroses, in addictions, power mad displays of enthusiasm, banality, diversions of increasing urgency, and more and more loneliness. The gods have hardly departed; they have simply gone underground and reappear as wounds, as inflations, as pathologies. Our contemporary suffering is not tragic, for we wrestle not with gods; rather it is pathetic, the suffering which is unconscious and invariably victimizing of self and others.

How will it end? As it always ends, with the hubris humbled and the suppliant soul opened to learn through suffering.

As Nietzsche has put it,

> There once was a star where some clever animals invented knowledge. It was the most arrogant and deceitful moment in the "history

---

[78] Ibid., p. 85.

of the world": but it lasted only a moment. Nature breathed in and out just a few times, then the star hardened and the clever animals had to die.[79]

What the gods ask of us is that we remember them, that we acknowledge their presence in every moment, even when we sleep, even when we are in motion, even when we think we are who we believe we are. To the omnipresent gods we are obliged to bring our recalcitrant soul, every day, in all its humiliations and petty triumphs, and confess,

> Your student, however slow, is willing,
> the only student you'll ever have.[80]

---

[79] Cited by Calasso, ibid., p. 184.
[80] Carl Dennis, "A Chance for the Soul," in *Practical Gods*, p. 31.

8
Psychopathology
What God Is Offended Here?

Is it because I do not pester you
with the invisible gnats of meaning,
never release the whippets of anxiety
    from their crates,
or hold up my monstrous mirror,
a thing the size of a playing field?
—Billy Collins, "The Flight of the Reader."

Modern psychotherapy and psychiatry is dominated by the
DSM-IV, our loving abbreviation of the *Diagnostic and Statistical Manual, Fourth Edition*. No trainee in any program from
psychiatry to social work learns anything about the gods, but
they all have to know the *DSM-IV*, the therapeutic Bible, as it
were.

Each is taught to diagnose by number, to observe behaviors,
collect history and match it all up with a designation which was
reached by committee consensus after, for sure, both conflict
and compromise. According to the *DSM-IV*, we no longer suffer
that common cold called depression but have a "dysthymic disorder," dysthymic being a word from the Greek which means an
absence of strong feeling. (Even the *DSM-IV* unwittingly suc-
cumbs to metaphor).

Thus one is without ardor, Aphrodite is banished, Ares repressed and so on. There is no particular concern for etiology,
for causal factors, and there is no particular concern for out-
comes, as that will be the subject of a treatment plan, influenced
increasingly by insurance companies and their managerial lack-

eys. And, be assured, there is no mention of which god is offended here in our beloved *DSM-IV*.

While there is a noble effort at work in the *DSM-IV* and all its predecessors, an honorable effort to find universal behavioral patterns and reduce the chaos of diagnosis, medication regimens and treatment plans to facilitate uniformity of intention, terminology and professional communication, the net effect is the overgeneralization of the individual patient, the blurring of critical nuances of personality, and the removal of the depth dimension in service to that which can be observed, converted to a statistical norm and brought under the fantasy of control.

The motive is consciously good, and unconsciously distracting if not often harmful. Therapist and patients are obliged to serve this model if they wish to communicate with others, be admitted to a clinic, receive insurance payments, prescriptions and so on. It is a managerial system, well intended, but ultimately demeaning to the individual and to the telluric powers which drive the soul. Most of all, one is never permitted to mention a suspect, amorphous word like *soul*, which as I've noted is what *psyche* means in the original Greek.

Like any riddle, the one word which may not be mentioned is, of course, the answer to the conundrum.

Let us take a brief foray into the *DSM-IV* and find what awaits us there. For one thing, our old, familiar companion *depression* has virtually vanished, as mentioned above. Whatever has been "pressed backward or downward" is now suffering from insufficient ardor or élan, and well it should. Depression which arises from an intrapsychic as opposed to a biological source, is an autonomous withdrawal of libido from its investment in the outer world. The ego may renew its investments in the old goals, but the libido refuses to go where the ego wishes. In short, the person is up against some power transcendent to the ego.

It certainly would be peculiar to call such a power a god,

wouldn't it? Yet Jung made an audacious statement back in November of 1959 in a letter to Valentine Brooke. He is responding to all the queries which came his way after stating in the famous BBC television interview with John Freeman that he did not need to believe in God, because he knew![81] Many people wrote to Jung to ask him to clarify what he meant by this statement. His reply is provocative, and well worth our attention:

> I know of the existence of God-images in general and in particular. I know it is a matter of a universal experience and, in so far as I am no exception, I know that I have such experience also, which I call God. It is the experience of my will over against another and very often stronger will, crossing my path often with seemingly disastrous results, putting strange ideas into my head and maneuvering my fate sometimes into most undesirable corners or giving it unexpected favorable twists, outside my knowledge and intention.[82]

To the obvious question, "Why call that God?" Jung replies,

> Why not? It has always been called "God." An excellent and very suitable name indeed. Who could say in earnest that his fate and life have been the conscious result of his conscious planning alone. . . .
> I know what I want, but I am doubtful and hesitant whether the Something is of the same opinion or not.[83]

For sure our sentimentality and our tendency toward anthropomorphosizing desires a more personable god; that is, *someone much more like us*, having of course the same moral values we espouse, and no doubt the same tastes in interior decoration, theories on how the world should be run, etc. But we can see from the vast pantheon of deities that many are without those personal characteristics which make us feel comfortable. Quite the contrary, they often confront us in brutal, impersonal ways.

---

[81] See McGuire amd Hull, eds., *C.G. Jung Speaking,* p. 428.
[82] *Letters,* vol. 2, pp. 522f.
[83] Ibid., p. 523.

What Jung is suggesting here is that whenever the ego's agenda is overthrown, whenever it is in the grip of transcendent powers, it is in the presence of divinity. That Something of whom, or of which, he speaks has an opinion, which has little in common with ours. If, for example, it were fully in accord with us, we would be immortal, beautiful, wise and omnipotent—none of which we are.

When we speak of "the gods" we are speaking metaphorically, as befits any approach to the *mysterium tremendum,* the great mystery. The gods are our personifications, please recall, the constructs of our limited intellects, which point toward the energies which run the cosmos and course through our being. So if one is "depressed," then our being is not consonant with the intention of the gods. The gods may very well take us anywhere they damn well wish, of course, including depression as a steady state. But when we examine the psychodynamics, that is, the dynamics of the soul, we discern that depression is the expression of an energy transcendent to the ego's choices, albeit felt as an oppression.

Perhaps the ego is under the influence of a complex (which is a split-off mythologem, sometimes even an entire mythological system), or is lacking in a range of imaginal choices, as so often happens to us in childhood. A child may be depressed simply because the range of options open to it, either literally or imaginally, are dystonic with the developmental agenda of the gods.

Or consider anxiety, that steady-state affect of our existential, precarious existence. It is hard to imagine an organism which experiences equanimity in the face of its imminent annihilation, although that counterpoise has been the chief goal of most world religions. Many of those religions seek surcease of suffering through sleight of hand, the promise of an afterlife, which after all is simply offering the ego the promise of a second go at it, presumably under better conditions. Perhaps only Buddhism seeks the most difficult, namely the release of anxiety by an act of ego itself. To that one would have to add the great moral force of the Twelve Step programs in their many efforts to recognize and accede to the limits of effort.

Just recently I spoke with a colleague who was anguishing over the plight of her adult son and daughter, both of whom she was still supporting and protecting. As natural as her emotional attachment to her children is, she is exhausted by both her work and the prolongation of parenting, for the great human wave of dependency and neediness has no end. Holding back such a sea is clearly hopeless. Yet those who have been raised in chaotic, unstable environments have learned to sacrifice their own needs, and the promptings of their own soul, in service to the fantasy of stabilizing their surroundings. They are left with chronic feelings of guilt over failure to do so, anger at being obliged to do so (which usually masquerades as depression, "anger turned inward"), and an exhausting, frantic agenda for fixing the world.

In our discussion, I had to rehearse for her what she well knew, but needed to hear again, namely the realistic limits of her powers, the fact that her children and her patients were also in the hands of the gods, and that the gods run the cosmos without seeking our advice and consent. There was a mutual lowering of anxiety once these reminding words were spoken. No great insight. No revolution of personality. Simply a reminder that the gods are in charge, not humans. With this reminder we may either have the level of our anxiety raised, or we will be somewhat more able to walk away from it. The offense against the gods which anxiety embodies, then, is to forget that the gods are the gods. We sometimes think we are, and that is enough to make anyone anxious.

The current scandals of clerical pedophilia and child abduction remind us that each of us may be stuck in service to a single, early mythologem that arrests the developmental course of eros.

It is easy to despise the other who has committed grievous wrong against the vulnerable, without recognizing that our own eros has its pernicious permutations which will out one way or another. There is an old German proverb: "Write the Devil's name on the wall, and He will appear." Banish the thought, and the god will seek revenge in some other venue.

Pathology after all means "the expression of suffering." A wounding of the god is a pathology in which we are all complicit. The gods are not moral in the conventional sense of which we usually speak. The shark which swallows us, the tornado that destroys our home, the cancer which eats us, is not moral at all; it simply is *Dasein*, being as is, a "just-so" story. Yet, if we are to live within any sort of community, we are morally responsible for all our services to the gods.

The most dangerous person, as the daily news illustrates, is the person in denial of the erotic energy which courses through the soul. Therefore, the godly energy perforce will be acted out. The milky theologies on which so many of us were raised ignore the implacable, sometimes destructive and always imperious character of divinity. Such gods denied seek revenge through the unconscious. In the case of one person the crime will be against the innocent and vulnerable child; in another the crime will be against oneself through the repression, perhaps somatization, of the energy into atrophied eros.

When we examine the *DSM-IV* we find many categories of human experience, all of them described in behavioral forms, just as most if not all colleges now feature departments of Social and Behavioral Sciences. (Next to business majors, they are the most subscribed by students, while the least subscribed are languages, fine arts, history.) Who would argue that behaviors are unimportant? Certainly I don't. Our history is in part the sum of our behaviors. And yet, our history is also a genetic pattern unfolding, an archetypal process following its developmental agenda, a series of choices which may or may not be conscious, and beyond that, something mysterious of which we have little knowledge and even less control. When we total the sum of these factors, something is always missing, the cipher for the mystery we call the gods.

Among the behavioral categories most commonly encountered in the *DSM-IV* are the addictions and the paraphilias (fancy word for sexual disorders). Could there be a connection between these subscription patterns, one in the pattern of college majors, one in these popular pathologies? On the surface there is no connection, but perhaps the gods are at work in these mysterious places as well. Given that our so-called social sciences are driven to be logical, rigorous and above all measurable, could it be that the gods are simply driven underground and become, as Jung says, "diseases"?

What is it that addictions and paraphilias have in common? Both are urgent, insistent compulsions. No one awakes in the morning and seeks to ruin the day. No one invites unwanted, often unconscious, thoughts, or obsessions; no one wants to be at the mercy of compulsions, acts whose motive is the amelioration of the angst occasioned by those throbbing thoughts. What they have in common, of course, is the desire for connection. (Moreover, this desire for connection is, we recall, buried in the etymology of our word *religion*, which means "to bind back to or reconnect with.") Our common condition is one of separation, the Fall, the loss, the expulsion from the womb, and the subsequent experience of a lonely, perilous wandering through an often hostile world, delaying only awhile the inevitable conclusion: annihilation. (And, oh yes, have a nice day!)

The desire for connection is symbolically transferred to food (matter/Mater), acquisitions, alcohol (the *aqua vitae* or *spiritus*), work, a warm body. In every case the existential longing is transferred to a surrogate and the symbol is reified into an obsession followed by a palliative behavior or compulsion. The healing of the archetypal wound is of course only transitory and thus must be repeated; that is its addictive quality.

Addictions are common to all humans. One needs only to look for the repetitive anxiety management techniques which are employed on reflexive basis in the conduct of daily life. The question is not whether addiction, but which addiction, taking what symbolic form, to what degree of effectiveness, and having what magnitude of consequences. As for the paraphilias, here again the APA (American Psychiatric Association) has recourse to metaphor. The word suggests the "all-loving permutations of our yearning," a yearning which only connection with the gods could possibly satisfy.

We all yearn from a split soul. One part longs to cling to the earth in chthonic embrace; the other yearns for the heavens, for transcendence, for spiritual homecoming. Thus we see in the most common forms of psychopathology—addictions and paraphilias—a longing for connection with the lost divinities, the sources of life, progenitors of our energy systems, repositories of meaning—the home from which we are all separated and toward which our soul naturally wends.

Until we can "name" the god for whom we long, and acknowledge the power of our hunger in the economy of our daily life, we can only manipulate behaviors, reinforce shaky ego strength, experience relapse, compulsions and guilt. Until one can surrender consciously to the longing for the gods, one will be stuck in the mire of the material, the barren plain of behavioral modification fantasies, and the denigration of the human soul.

Rather than recover the respect for the mysteries, our contemporary psychiatric attitudes drive them further from our purview. And thus we get sicker, and our culture more desperate.

No wonder, then, that so many suffer from eating disorders, for we hunger for the gods, or alternatively seek to control our continued estrangement from the ground of our being. We also observe the proliferation of dissociative disorders as well, for who can bear to stay in an untenable reality, a place where the integrity of one's soul is violated? Who would not wish to go to a place where the soul is protected? Even in the most extreme dissociative disorders, such as fugue and amnesia or Dissociative Identity Disorders, we notice how the Self partitions itself, autonomously, in order to preserve itself.

When we cannot stand in right relationship to our souls, something inside us acts to protect us. So often the *DSM-IV,* and those obliged to utilize its descriptions, encapsulate their clients in diagnoses that are implicitly judgmental and diminishing. The worth and depth of each individual soul, the independence of spirit, and the separate path of individuation which each of us is summoned to tread, is sacrificed in service to the fantasy of denomination, control and alteration. But the gods will not be mocked and only more pathologizing of both client and therapist results.

Yet, paradoxically, if the gods are diseases, then our diseases are religious. If the gods are personifications of the forces which run the universe, then our disorders are violations of those energies and their teleological intentions for us.

Another category of rising diagnostic incidence is today called "personality disorders." Formerly called characterological disorders, as if they were failures of character through not living up to some collective sense of morality, personality disorders are failures of "personhood." Here again we have metaphor at work, even from the APA. Some Jungian theorists call these phenomena "disorders of the Self," suggesting that the relationship to the Self has been damaged, often by family of origin or cultural trauma. This is a rather useful metaphor as long as one is willing to equate the activity of the Self with the teleology of the gods. I, for one, am willing to make such a metaphoric equation.

Indeed, the Self itself is a metaphor. It is not an entity; it is an activity. The Self *selves*; the gods *god*, as it were. (Notice how difficult it is in our denominative language to turn these nouns into their proper identity as verbs. One sounds awkward, even ridiculous in so doing, but we must make the effort to recover the dynamic, teleological yet unpredictable character of the gods at their godly work.)

Of course I have not been fair to the APA and the *DSM-IV*, for their intent is serious, conscientious and, given the bureaucratization of our mental health services, perhaps even unavoidable. Forgive me for a degree of rhetorical hyperbole, but do allow the point to be made nonetheless. I ask that we not be bewitched by this diagnostic language, by this pseudo-scientific nomenclature, this tome, this therapeutic Torah, as so many practitioners are, as so many insurance companies insist, and through which so many folks are unfortunately diminished, condescended to and labeled for a lifetime.

There is no prescription for our common condition, no Prozac for the personality, no Serentil for the soul's surcease, no Respiradol for spiritual respite, no escape from our anomie. When the inner myth and the outer myth do not line up, then we are divided souls. When the outer myth does not support individuation, then we are living an existential dissociation. Such is the climate and the context of our time, and that is why depth psychology had to be invented in the late nineteenth century.

By the end of the nineteenth century, the human soul had fallen into the gap between the medical model, wonderful and useful as it is, and the ecclesiastical model, as constrictive as it had become. Someone had to walk into those depths in search of the soul, to track the gods to their ancient lair. Freud and Jung, and others who followed, made that step into the inner abyss because they had to. Not only did their patients need them, but they had to do so for their own souls' sake as well. The fading relevance of tribal mythology led them to search for the source of all myth, the dynamic psyche, residence of the gods and arena of their enactments.

Psychoanalysis is not a surrogate religion, as some have charged. Nevertheless, its work may lead one to recover a sense of awe at the movement of transcendent forces within. As we know, institutional religion can often be a defense against the possibility of religious experience. And much of modern psychotherapy is a defense against the possibility of true psychological encounter, practiced by those who have never had one hour of personal analysis. What if one took the psyche seriously? Then one would have to acknowledge the presence of what we metaphorically call *the gods*; then one might have to relinquish the fantasy of control, management and resolution of the raggedy mysteries of our journey.

The real work of therapy is to approach the numinous, to be awed again, frightened, uplifted by it as we were as children, and to experience the will of the gods at work in our bones, our dreams and, perhaps, through the enlargement of consciousness.

9
Our Stories as Our Personal Myth

A man finds his shipwrecks,
tells himself the necessary stories.
Whatever gods are—our own fearful voices
or intimations from the unseen order
of things . . . .
— Stephen Dunn, "Odysseus's Secret."

The invisible world governs the visible world, which is one of the
reasons why it is so difficult to be wholly, or even partly, conscious. Every life is the enactment of not one story, but many.
The story we consciously know, or believe we know, is seldom
the whole story which is unfolding within us.

Our stories go deep, very deep, into the archetypal realm, into
the genetic code, the tribal history, the family of origin, both
known and repressed, as well as the mythologies we live out on a
daily basis—the complexes. Each complex is a fractal of a whole
world view, a value system and a sequence of programmed somatic and affective responses.

When any given complex is active, for example, one is playing out an old story of the rejected child, of daddy's favorite, of
mother's hope or sibling's resentment. When we are in the grip
of a complex we are always in the past, the place of origin, and
in the warp and weft of value systems of which we are only
dimly aware, if at all.

As a Jungian analyst, my daily vocation is to read surfaces—
what we say, what we do not say, what the body says, what the
behavioral pattern attests, what the dream images intimate, and
so on. It is strange, difficult, even alienating work at times,

shrouded in secrecy and wrapped in a curious mix of mystery, terror and wonder.

So often I have found, as every analyst finds, that our stories are living us rather than we creating them. So much for ego sovereignty. To truly realize that there is a genetic code, a family mythos, and clusters of psychic energy living through us, is humbling to say the least. Grudgingly we learn that there are conscious stories and unconscious stories which embody themselves through us every day, as well as archetypal stories of the species of which we are but a small though unique carrier.

To ask, what is your story? is to be obliged to ask what are your *stories,* for we are no single narrative. What is humbling is the acknowledgment through age, repetition and the growth of consciousness that we have less autonomy in the construction of our lives than we had fantasized. In the end, the chief result of a long-term analysis is not a solution to our dilemma, for life is not a problem, but a progressive unfolding of mystery. The joyful discovery is that our lives become more interesting to us as we discern that we are part of a larger mystery. This is a proper relocation of the ego from its imperial fantasy to its unique, personal place. We become amazed witnesses of the great theater wherein we play our part, and are reminded of the   progressive incarnation which occurs in even the most modest of moments.

The revelation that our story will prove interesting to us seems a modest hope in the face of unremitting suffering, but it is what is most meaningful about our brief sojourn on this earth. No mosaic is complete without its separate, brilliant fragments. To recognize the stories which are living us is to recover the magnitude of wonder we had in childhood.

It begins in wonder

When I visited my four-year-old grandson recently he peppered me with questions. (His mother reports that it is a nightmare to entice him out of the hardware store). He is full of questions because he is full of wonder as the world unfolds for him. He not only asks how things work, but why, why, why. That is one kind of questioning which our psyche still asks, even if our consciousness has become dulled and locked into repetitions.

One of the few moderns who continued to ask childlike questions so elementary that they open profound abysses before us was Ludwig Wittgenstein. He could ask not only why a phenomenon might occur, but how we could observe it and convert it to something inside us. Such queries always stumble at first on the conventions through which we apprehend the world, but in the end lead to wonder that it and we exist at all.

Many times, however, the flavor and meaning of our life is really wrapped around specific questions. In *On This Journey We Call Our Life* I sought to identify ten such questions as are worthy of our journey, believing that if we do not ask large questions, our lives will be small. But we must also consider some of the less conscious, smaller questions that govern our lives.

"How can I become secure?" Such a question can only beget more insecurity, for whatever comfort we choose to address that question—more money, the right partner, a predictable God—will only provide ever more insecurity since our assigned security can never really prove secure. If we ask, "How can I find a partner to meet my needs?" we are, through the potential for controlling the other implicit in that question, as well as their inherent separateness, already destroying the relationship to which we look for narcissistic fulfillment.

If one asks, "How can I make people respect me, or like me?", then one's uncertain relationship to the Self will repeatedly undermine our conscious intention and produce an atmosphere in which our doubt of ourselves will arouse doubt in others. Living out such a question will make one act as a mere performer who lives only for the perceived tastes of others.

If one's question is, "How do I avoid offending God?" chances are we have offended God most by deflecting our individuation, by sabotaging the project we are. Usually the implicit, and sometimes explicit, question of our family of origin became ours as well, and rare is the person who has truly transcended the power of such an unconscious mythological engine.

When I was my grandson's age, and I can identify that moment from the place where we lived, I recall asking another question. I sat in the grass and looked at the skies. I thought—to use a language common to the adult—that the sky formed an oval, a cell as it were, which was one cell in the brain of a giant thinker, a god, and that I and the world I knew were a thought, perhaps a dream of that great thinker.

It simultaneously occurred to me that said thinker or dreamer might have another thought, another dream, and I would disappear. I did not tell anyone of these musings for I feared ridicule, or perhaps that I was venturing into some forbidden zone as I did when I first learned about "sex" by innocently singing a ditty another child had taught me. Such matters were not to be approached, it was clear. Sex became numinous in that very moment. It was during World War Two and I came home joyously singing through the neighborhood at the top of my lungs: "Lost my arm in the army, / lost my leg in the navy, / lost my balls in Niagara Falls, / and found them in the gravy." I also sang (since you asked): "Whistle while you work, / Hitler is a jerk, / Mussolini bit his weenie, / now it doesn't work."

I thought these songs appealing, not because I understood the vocabulary but because they rhymed. I quickly learned that one does not forage in such regions, an admonition I soon prudently extended to theological speculations as well.

In those days we fantasized that someone would take us aside and tell us the meaning of this journey. Life loomed large, the body fell into anarchy, society demanded, and we complied.

Now, all these years later, with all the wrecks on the highway, all the carnage of the heart, we still do not know the answer to Agee's question, to Rilke's question. If we shun consciousness, with its painful gift of responsibility, we may wish to blame others, even though the only person present in all the scenes of this long-running soap opera is ourselves. Possibly, then, we might have had something to do with all this; possibly it matters to discern which myths we have been living out.

By now you know that your parents gave up the search, stopped asking questions. The brittle teachers, the clerics in bad hair-dos, the preening politicians, all did the same. In fact, no one has the answers, not then, not during, not now. Your story courses through you nonetheless, making choices for you, creating history, inviting futures. What is not conscious owns you, and very little is conscious, even to those who try. More than making our story, our story is making us.

What we ignore of the myth unfolding within us will surely come to us, or appear to come to us, as Jung repeatedly suggests, as if it were the ministry of Fate. For example, our relational imagoes, the sense of self, sense of other, and scenario for reenactment, will tend to cause one to chose the same sort of person over and over, rehearse earlier dynamics, and come to similar conclusions.[84]

Or we may find ourselves repeatedly bumping up against the limits of choice which constricted our family of origin. We either silently conform to those limits and thereby undermine our individuation project, or spend enormous amounts of energy seeking to overcompensate for those limits, thus unwittingly producing other distortions of our myth.

---

[84] See Hollis, *The Eden Project: In Search of the Magical Other,* for an extended discussion of the patterns of our relationships

How did the story get lost?

> O lost, and by the wind grieved, ghost, come back again.
> —Thomas Wolfe, *Look Homeward Angel.*

> What seest thou else
> In the dark backward and abysm of time?
> —William Shakespeare, *The Tempest.*

How much, then, is present choice, driven by "the dark backward and abysm of time," and how did our story get lost in the first place?

It is part of our intuitive knowing as children that we were sent here with a story given by the gods. How we enact that story, suffering the various crucifixions of the ego's desire for comfort and security along the way, is what Jung means by the mythologem of *individuation.* Individuation, too often confused with individualism and with its attendant narcissism and self-infatuation, is rather more often an ordeal of summons, angst, false turns and humiliation before the gods.

The violation of this personal myth will lead to pathologies of various sorts, suffering by ourselves and/or those around us. Such unwitting betrayal will wound the body, self and other, and cause that splitting we call "neurosis." The flight from the summons of the gods is the chief pathology of our time and all of us have fallen into it

In the womb the eyes did not see, the lungs did not breathe—we floated timelessly through inner space. Time, consciousness, can only be engendered at birth. No wonder that the myth which stands at the beginning of almost all peoples is the loss of paradise, that is, primal connection, and the fall into consciousness made possible only through this loss.

While much of our identity is genetically and culturally conditioned, it is fair to observe that we have all experienced the twin woundings of overwhelment and abandonment. Given the magnitude, extent and duration of these existential events, we fashion coping strategies through trial and error, based at best on partial readings of the world. While life will bring us other interpretations, other experiences of relationship, other strengths, few paradigms of self and world are more powerful than those which come to us when we are most vulnerable, most impressionable, least capable of discerning alternatives, least able to reflect.

Accordingly, how can we claim to live our stories when these distorting lenses and anxiety management strategies prevail? This unavoidable collision of nature and nurture, of soul and environment, is how we lose contact with our personal myth and fall into someone else's. Our lives are spent, then, serving competing mythologies, one given by the gods, the other acquired through our interpretations of the world. We are a divided country, strangers to ourselves.

The old Zen admonition to look for the face we had before the world was made is a recollection of our primal myth. Yet our stories are incoherent and broken. We may even be minor characters in this story we call our life. Sometimes we are only bystanders, waiting around till the end to see what the novel was about—a story so brief, so fragile, so tainted. And too often we find that we have lived someone else's life, someone else's story.

Stories of stories

It might prove illuminating to reflect on some other person's narrative. Franz Kafka wrote his story as much out of his wounds as anyone ever did. He wrote to save himself, to express his profound insight, and to find some relief. But there was none.

In the short story, "The Judgment," for example, Kafka illustrates the power of a core complex, in this case the negative father complex. Recall that the value system—the charged affect and the bond to history—is usually primitive, phenomenological and experiential.

The archetypal father imago serves as a mythologem for the task of agency, namely the degree to which we can feel our own worth and psychological *gravitas*. We must create a way to exercise our powers in service to the soul. If one feels support for the legitimacy of this endeavor and the courage to enact it, then one is serving the positive father mythologem. If consciously or unconsciously one believes that one is inadequate to the task, then the energic charge is a negative one. It is incumbent upon us to reflect on which kind of energy rules our story. (The charging of the mythologem is only partially the consequence of the actual father experience, and is reinforced or contradicted by other cultural and relational experiences).

Just as Jung described a complex as a splinter personality, so too can we see such complexes as splinter mythologies, activated by conscious or unconscious stimuli, playing out their archaic program, recreating our identities for distant times and places.

Living as he did with a critical, demanding father, Kafka's personal journey was diverted into withstanding the impact of a larger force than he. He extrapolated the encounter with the life-denying father to the god of his people's patriarchal religion. He obtained a doctorate of law but made his living computing actuarial tables for a worker's insurance company.

In "The Judgment," a young man has been writing to a pen pal in Russia. To an East European, Russia at the beginning of the last century would have implied a summons to adventure and discovery, much as the North American west once did. The pen pal urges him to leave Prague and come to Russia to start a new life. The father finds the letter and says to the youth, "I sentence you now to death by drowning!"[85]

Obediently, the young man walks through the streets of Prague, crosses a bridge and jumps into the river below. The conclu-

---

[85] *Selected Short Stories*, p. 18.

sion is shocking, even unbelievable. We wish to say, "But that is not true to life!" One would not destroy one's life so casually, we say; no one has such power over another. Yet many of us live out such core mythologies, destroy our own possibilities by avoidance or self-defeating behaviors. Such a disempowering mythologem is the enemy of life, the opponent of risk and venture, the denial of our story.

All of us have some such complex at work, albeit in varying degrees of magnitude. Who has not drowned in the insurgent waters of the unconscious? Wheresoever we have denied our possibilities, colluded with fear, denigrated our personal aspirations, conspired Quisling-like with our invader, we have known the power of such negative father energy. For all his brilliance, Kafka knew that power well; it dominated his life. He knew he could never escape its judgment, and that behind the father stood the *imago Dei*, the stern, judgmental Yahweh from whose piercing glare no human may hide.

In Kafka's short story "The Metamorphosis," the central character, Gregor Samsa, awakens one morning to find he has become a giant insect.[86] He is bewildered, disoriented, still thinking about getting to work on time. His family is repulsed, rejecting. Nothing changed there, for they have "bugged" him for a long time. They find him an embarrassment and pelt him with apples. Despite the preposterous character of the metaphor, Kafka again portrays the deformation of the personal myth through the power of the complex. He has experienced, and can communicate, a metaphor to embody the dilemma of radical depersonalization.

In "A Hunger Artist," Kafka depicts a circus performer whose talent is fasting.[87] He fasts, and has made an art of it. For awhile

---

[86] Ibid., pp. 19ff.
[87] Ibid., pp. 188ff.

people are curious and come to watch him not eat, but they assume he snacks surreptitiously. Soon there are more intriguing acts on the scene and attendance slumps. When he is asked why he does not eat, the hunger artist replies that he would gladly have eaten had he ever found something he wanted.

How many of us have wasted away in some vital area of our calling, simply because nothing nourishing was ever offered us?

Slowly the hunger artist wastes away. He ends up as a heap of clothing in the cage, and is replaced by a hungry tiger. The crowds come back to see this amusement which distracts them from their own hunger.

Again we see the dramatization of a powerful complex with its archaic fantasy. Kafka did not find the sustenance his soul desired, but he learned to make an art of his want, an enduring portrait of his and our emotional starvation. The child not fed can only operate within the sphere of its experience, often concluding that it is unworthy to be fed and that life itself offers no nourishment.

"A Hunger Artist" can be seen as Kafka's personal confession. He suffered the life-denying power of a core introject, the negative father who enclosed him on all sides, and he endured a life of emotional starvation. To his credit, he turned his suffering into profound expression even as he remained under the sway of this destructive mythos. Before tuberculosis consumed him at age thirty-nine, he created a body of work which speaks of the spiritual poverty of our entire age. Our appreciation of it does not prevent us from wishing that he might have found sustenance nonetheless.[88]

Kafka's contemporary and fellow countryman, Rilke, was originally named René, made to dress as a girl, and told by his

---

[88] For a study of the effect of Kafka's mother complex, see Daryl Sharp, *The Secret Raven: Conflict and Transformation in the Life of Franz Kafka.*

mother that he was a poor surrogate for his sister who had died before him. As an adult, his relationships with women were tumultuous and transient. He once wrote that he could not love a woman because he could not love his mother. He also wrote that he had built his defenses against her, only to watch her invade and occupy him. With such a paradigm for relating to the feminine, how could the adult have any other course for his own life?

Again, Rilke was a brilliant, insightful person, but even this gifted soul could not escape the power of his intrapsychic imago. Unnurtured by the archetypal feminine, his hold on life was too delicate. Like a flower too fragile for the world, he too died prematurely, after the pinprick of a rose complicated his leukemia. His epitaph was to a rose, which, in its complicated, unfolding layers, embodied the exquisite beauty of the mystery. Suffering the depredations of incursion, he wrote some of the most sensitive lyrics of the twentieth century, poems of great longing and tenderness, yet could not abide the comfort of a companion.

The story of the celebrated poet Silvia Plath is similarly informed by core complexes. Her mother, a Southern woman of some considerable talent, but professionally frustrated, lived through her daughter. Her ambivalence and jealousy burdened her child with her own unlived life. But Sylvia's most famous poem, "Daddy," tells another story. Her father was a New England professor. In her poem he is portrayed as a depraved monster, compared to Dracula and to a Nazi. One is led to suspect massive damage here, surely child molestation, given the affective magnitude of the metaphors.

By report, Otto Plath was just a normal neurotic like most of us, albeit fastidious and demanding, but not an odious monster. His daughter Sylvia, who in the poem likens herself to a victim of a Nazi concentration camp, has no right to such an invidious comparison. When she later gassed herself, she was both victim and perpetrator, and deliberately chose to pay the shilling to light the flame. The children on the boxcars to the various camps had no such choice, and their memory must not be lessened by cheap comparisons. Still, the metaphor, like Kafka's bugdom, must be respected. But what could account for the magnitude of it?

In "Daddy," Plath alludes to her previous suicide attempts when she attempted to "get back" at him. On the one hand she has the manipulative mother living her life through her child, pushing her toward stardom while sticking a leg out to make her fall, and then managing her daughter's career toward cultic celebrity after her suicide. On the other hand, she lived with this relatively arid, nonempowering father who had the bad taste to die when Sylvia was ten. His monstrous "crime," then, was not molestation, it was abandonment. So, carrying the negative, critical demanding father within, abandoned by the hope for nurturance, carrying the mother's ambivalent ambitions, Sylvia repeatedly attempts to end her pain by psychotic breaks and suicide. There is no safe place to go, no nurturant ground. Finally, when a baby sitter is overdue to relieve her in London, she is found with her head in the oven.

"Daddy" remains a powerful indictment. It is not a poem as much as a *cri de coeur*. It is more emotional purgation than poetry. It is less a Wordsworthian "emotion recollected in tranquility,"[89] than catharsis of black bile. But most of all, it is a troubling reminder of the power of the core mythologems with their terrible engines at work in our lives. This bright, gifted girl, this child of troubled parents who were themselves someone else's children, could not stop being the child of her parents. And how many of us ever do?

Two other brief examples, both presidents of the United

---

[89] "Preface to Second Edition of Lyrical Ballads (1800)," in *William Wordsworth: The Major Works,* p. 8.

States: Abraham Lincoln and William Jefferson ("Bill") Clinton. Both rose to enormous power from impoverished origins. Both were driven, eloquent, intellectually gifted men with massive mother complexes. For all their gifts, both suffered greatly from this core issue. The power of the archaic imago can hardly be overemphasized, both in its capacity to replicate the past and its staying power. Despite commanding vast armies, both men remained in service to their mothers throughout their lives.

We all know Lincoln as the great gray wisdom, brooding over the injustice of slavery and attending the most horrific of civil bloodletting. He left political life in 1849 after an unremarkable political career. For five years he practiced law in Springfield, rode the southern Illinois circuit, supported his family, and then, after a debilitating midlife depression, returned to politics with new vigor. His depression certainly seems to fit what has been called a creative crisis, the collision of the provisional personality with the insurgency of the Self. If a person can come through such a *catabasis*, he or she is renewed and enlarged. New parts of the personality are engaged. The false self is challenged. Renewing energy arises from an inner source.

But Lincoln's life was still dominated by the negative anima. His father had been emotionally distant, his mother stern and critical but supportive. His adaptation to the masculine energy was necessarily skewed by the absent father. The one love of his life, Anne Rutledge, died of fever back in New Salem. When he married it seemed more out of resignation than anything else. His wife, Mary Todd, would today likely be diagnosed as suffering a bipolar disorder. She had deep, dark depressions, spent considerable time in a mental hospital after being placed there by her surviving son, was jealous of others, a spendthrift who went on ruinous buying sprees, and was emotionally and physically abusive to President Lincoln. Many times in Springfield, Lincoln was observed sleeping outside as he sought to avoid her. She threw tantrums in the White House and in public and was a general embarrassment to all. But the Commander-in-Chief of the world's largest army at the time was powerless before her. Lincoln considered his marriage hell, but it was a necessary hell before which he was incapacitated. Accordingly, we see that he reenacts in his marriage the absent masculine and the negative feminine. That which seems most intransigent, least susceptible to the alterations of consciousness, derives from the core mythologem. Lincoln experienced his marriage as "a fountain of misery, of a quality absolutely infernal."[90] His mother, whom he publically called an angel, was cruel to him and often beat him. Locally she had a reputation for immorality. His relationships with women in general were notable for his passivity. But, given the fact that his mother died when he was nine, he was also terrified by the thought of abandonment, for whatever else she was, that mother was the only source of warmth in the child's life. Little doubt, then, that he would find a woman like Mary Todd who was more than domineering in her emotional instability, and before whom he was powerless and yet fearful of losing her. *Plus ça change, plus c'est la même chose.*

Bill Clinton shares a similar background: a missing father, a dominating, sometimes unstable mother, whom he both worships and fears, and an inability to transcend the paradigm. He marries a dominating woman and engages in compulsive affairs, bringing his life to the edge of ruin. This pattern suggests the dual need to be subservient and yet compulsively connect with the feminine to achieve reassurance over the threat of abandonment.

The origin of any obsession is a deep-seated anxiety for which the compulsion is intended as a palliative treatment. Like his predecessor Richard Nixon, who experienced the same structure, and who recalled his mother on the day of his exile from the

---

[90] Michael Burlingame, *The Inner World of Abraham Lincoln*, p. 268.

White House, Clinton's own choices brought him to grief. Neither Nixon nor Clinton seemed to have been able to reflect on the pattern and to recognize from whence sprang their choices. This silent hand of fate internalized is the stuff of tragedy. In classic Greek tragedy, of course, the protagonist, through suffering, comes to wisdom. But in day to day life, it always remains to be seen whether one can and will go through the redemptive suffering that leads to knowledge and healing.

The one question none of us can answer is: of what are we unconscious? Nonetheless, a good faith analysis of the patterns of one's life can often lead to the discovery of the hidden factors of which our outer patterns are in fact a logical extension.

The worst thing we can do to others is burden them with our unconscious material, and yet we cannot avoid doing so. It stands to reason, then, that the best we can do in our relationships is make our inner story more conscious. For all of us, history is what we have done as a result of being unconscious. What drives each of us to do what we have done is what makes history; rarely is our history the unfolding of fully conscious intentions. Fate's wounding flies toward repetition in a thousand guises.

While it may offend some to consider a complex a mythology, several important ideas become clearer when we do. First, as the mythos which each complex embodies is historically generated, so its activation and seizure of consciousness obliges the imposition of a prior sense of self and world upon the present. Secondly, the dynamics of such mythologies have a reflexive tendency toward the repetition compulsion and therefore the creation and reinforcement of a pattern, which, chosen or not, becomes our fate. Thirdly, the power of the mythologems therein have the potential to extend beyond the confines of the present. They can contaminate, for good or ill, our broader relationships to the world. As the core complex speaks, so our dialogue with the world is influenced by the meaning cluster which is

at the center. Fundamental attitudes such as trust/distrust, de-
pendence/independence, capacity for intimacy/sociophobia, and
so on ripple out from the mythic core.

Lastly, the energy at the core of the mythological system is
our energy; it is a scintilla of the soul. Whenever it may be as-
similated more fully into consciousness, it has the power to enlarge our frame of reference and our scope of action. It is the
secret sea from which all our life springs, and without which we
are not ourselves. It is our fragmentary glimpse of the gods.

10
The Recovery of Mystery in a Sterile Time

Only mystery enables us to live.
—Garcia Lorca.

Not I, not I, but the wind that blows through me.
—D. H. Lawrence.

It is wrong to say, "I think." One ought to say, "I am thought."
—Arthur Rimbaud.

What gods need is belief, and what humans want is gods.
—Terry Pratchet, *Small Gods.*

To live is to war with trolls in heart and soul.
—Henrik Ibsen.

The archives of our tribes are not so far gone that we do not remember a time when they were connected directly to the gods.

On this day I have watched the rescue of nine miners from a Pennsylvania cave-in. After several days in water, 240 feet below the surface, their rescue was surprising, stunning and, yes, miraculous. They were not abandoned by their colleagues, their families prayed and wept together, and guesses as to where to send the shafts of air to hold back the surging waters below and provide a modicum of heat were both scientific and fortuitous. Tonight, many gather in houses of worship to thank their God for deliverance. I would join them if I were there. Never mind the capriciousness of their God, nor the many who have perished on other days. They are alive; that is enough for this hour.

I agree with what Ovid wrote in his *Metamorphoses:* "Whom

the gods love are gods themselves, and those who have worshipped them should be worshipped too."[91] There is no evil here, merely the movement of those forces we call the gods. The great surge of nature stayed for now, they, we, are reserved for other deaths on other days. The apotropaisms of belief are celebrated in that little town tonight.

For most, however, the gods have fled and left a sterile world behind. Some have accommodated themselves stoically to stand with integrity in the presence of their absence. Poet Stephen Dunn writes directions to his eulogist:

> Tell them that at the end I had no need
> for God, who'd become just a story
> I once loved, one of many
> with concealments and late night rescues,
> high sentence and pomp. The truth is
> I'd learned to live without hope
> as well as I could, almost happily,
> in the despoiled and radiant now.[92]

The transition from the celestial city to the secular city has taken centuries. The radiant center of the Western world was already waning when Dante wrote the last great vision of metaphysical harmony, of moral cause and effect, and culminating in a soteriological fantasy. But the multifoliate rose which was his beatific vision of God was replaced by the machine, and then by the internet, and still other energies which shall go flashing into the dark. Wolfgang Koeppen describes this transition:

> Think of the strength that the attraction of heaven gave to people in the Middle Ages. . . . The donkey pulled the cart . . . heavenwards . . . but gradually the donkey realized that heaven was drawing no nearer, it grew tired, and the hay of religion no longer induced it.

---

[91] *Metamorphoses*, p. 198.
[92] "A Postmortem Guide," in *Different Hours,* pp. 120f.

. . . So, lest the cart come to a halt, the donkey's hunger was switched to an earthly paradise, a socialist park where all donkeys will be equal . . . but then the road to this Eden turns out to be just as long. . . . he wasn't pulling a cart but a carousel, and perhaps all we are is a sideshow on a fairground of the gods . . . only the gods have forgotten about us.[93]

When his companion opines that with such a view he would quickly commit suicide, he is told that he has no need to hurry toward extinction either way. If he were to have truth revealed, he fears he would not be able to sustain it. "There is something that is invisible to us, alongside the world and our lives. But what"?[94]

What is visible we know. Half the world lives awash in material abundance, and half below the poverty line. Half the world is addicted to something—power, food, wealth, substances which promise transformation. Both governments and corporations have forfeited the right to public trust. There is no company whose books one can fully trust, no government which is not riddled with mendacity.

Perhaps it has always been so, but the promises of materialism and progress have clearly failed to bring peace, salvation, spiritual comfort or very much meaning. If they did, we would see the evidence all around us; instead we see psychopathology, the suffering of the soul. We made gods of progress and materialism and other ideologies, and the gods, as Jung said, have become diseases.

And what have we become? According to T.S. Eliot we are the hollow men, headpiece filled with straw, and our voices are like rat's feet on broken glass in basements.[95] According to Robert

---

[93] *Death in Rome.* pp. 164f.
[94] Ibid., p. 166.
[95] "The Hollow Men," in *The Complete Poems and Plays: 1909-1950*, p. 56.

Musil in his 1930 novel, *The Man Without Qualities (Der Mann ohne Eigenshaften)* we have lost our souls, our individual personalities. What is a person without qualities, one asks?

> Nothing. That's just the point. . . . There are millions of them nowadays. . . . It's the human type our time has produced . . . [modern man] will look so generally intelligent that there is no single definite thing behind it at all.[96]

I would be inclined to translate the word *Eigenschaften* in this context as "characteristics," for a person without characteristics is ultimately a person without character, individuality, personhood. The texture of our time is to be *in between*—between, as Heidegger noted, the gods who have fled and the gods who have not yet arrived, between Pozzo and Lucky who wait for Godot, between Eichmann's "banality of evil," to use Hannah Arendt's phrase, and poet Carl Dennis, facing the question of his personal heaven or hell:

> Odds are I'll stay where I am, forever earthbound,
> And face the problem of filling the endless return
>
> Of earthly summers and autumns, winters and springs . . .
> A shadow too weak even to hold open a door.[97]

Ending, perhaps, with the lament of the Israeli poet-novelist Amos Oz:

> Only the sea is still there
> And even it has changed from deep blue
> To grey. Little boy don't believe. Or do. Believe. Who cares.[98]

The emergence of depth psychology over this past century plus is no accident. "Psychoanalysis," a term first used in a paper in 1896, has as its chief goal the holding of the tension of oppo-

---

[96] *The Man Without Qualities*, p. 70.
[97] "Eternal Life," lines 8-12, in *Practical Gods.*
[98] "Little Boy Don't Believe," in *The Same Sea*, p. 140.

sites during the great in-between—between phases of an individual's life, between old, presumed contracts with the universe, and newer, more complicated understandings, between the spiritual dispensations which nourished ancestors and the images which are available for us now. We have lost the sense of Ovid's vision where the connections to the invisible world were all around, where nature was a living testimony to the work of the gods. We have departed from the testimony of the Gnostic gospel which says that the kingdom is spread all over this earth yet we do not see it. We have lost the conviction of Marcus Aurelius:

> To those who insist, "Where have you ever seen the gods, and how can you be so assured of their existence, that you worship them in this way?" My answer is, "For one thing, they are perfectly visible to the eye." For another, "I have never seen my own soul either, but none the less I do venerate that. So it is with the gods; it is experience which proves their power every day, and therefore I am satisfied that they exist, and I do them reverence."[99]

We cannot have the direct experience which was available to the ancients. We must remember what the expression "the gods" means to those of us in the postmodern era. As Richard Tarnas puts it so succinctly, "Reality is understood to be pervaded and structured by powerful numinous forces and presences that are personified as mythic deities."[100]

Thus the gods are formed by our respect for the energic powers that course through the world. But we have come to recognize them as not only external but also as intrinsic archetypal aspects of our selves, as "primordial forms in the psyche that structure and impel human behavior and experience . . . expressions of a collective unconscious shared by all human beings."[101]

---

[99] *Meditations,* p. 186.
[100] *Prometheus the Awakener*, p. 4.
[101] Ibid.

Accordingly, for us to talk of the gods is to confess our distance from them, for we have turned them into nouns. But in remembering that they are not nouns, objects, but verbs, processes, we make a move toward recovery of the mystery. It is the dilemma of the modern to have to make this move, what William Blake called "reorganized innocence."

Such an innocence was the original state of those who had religious experience. Awed, they turned to metaphor, for what is truly transcendent cannot be contained within the general categories of mind and experience. Obviously, such metaphors have a tendency, when transferred to the experience of another, to reify, to become artifacts of consciousness rather than embodied experiential images.

The difficulty in transmitting original revelation leads to dogma, rites and cultic practices.

Dogma grows around an experience in order to explain it, to defend it, to communicate it to others. Obviously, the dogma as such bears no mystery, though it may speak in great sincerity of that original experience of it. Rituals have as their motive the recreation and, hopefully, the reanimation of the original experience, the *participation mystique* that accompanies phenomenological experience. In time, through reiteration, rituals can grow rigid and lose their capacity to reconnect a participant to the primal affect. Similarly, cultic practice, that which differentiates one tribal experience from another, can in time seem arbitrary.

As a result of the slippage of affective connection to the original image, institutions grow up around such experience in an effort to sustain the treasure which animated the elders.

As we all know, in time institutions may grow oppressive rather than expressive, imposing upon their communicants what seem arbitrary values and practices. And, in time, institutions gain a life of their own and their *raison d'être* evolves from keeping the fire to protecting its priesthood. All the while the gods have gone underground, only to appear elsewhere.

When we take the gods as *facts*, rather than metaphors, then we get lost in debating the merits of the facts rather than apprehending their meaning. The fundamentalist ties his or her beliefs to the facts and narrows the spiritual vitality by fighting rearguard actions against disputation. On the other hand, the atheist disputes the evidence, gets confused by the institutional forms to which he or she has been exposed, and misses the possible deepening which occurs whenever one confronts the meaning of divinity.

When institutions prevail over private experience, the oppression will manifest as depression and reification, precursors to the horrors of pogroms and crusades. This is the meaning behind the critiques of Kierkegaard and Nietzsche in the nineteenth century and the so-called "death of God" theologians in the twentieth. Each had observed that the *imago Dei* ossified and ceased to move its communicants to awe. In time, the momentum and self-interest of the institution can even serve to prevent people from primal, religious encounter which could actually threaten its stability and the social vision it guards.

As Jung said, the gods had become diseases. The names they once rendered luminous had become husks. As I have previously noted, the oldest of religious sins is to worship the husk after the energy has departed. It is called idolatry, and we have raised up many false gods in our time. Consider our contemporary Pantheon: plenipotentiary Progress, massive Materialism; heroic Health; normative Narcissism, nasty Nationalism; sophistic Scientism, and many others. None saves, none connects, none abides, and we all damn well know it.

It is not surprising then that psychodynamic psychology arose in the last decade of the nineteenth century to approach the yawning abyss which had opened in the human soul. For great masses of humanity the old institution offered nothing that truly moved the soul, and the new scientific paradigm, while providing great material advance, did not satisfy spiritual hunger.

When a god is denied, that is, when the energy which animates the universe and moves our soul is rejected, diverted, repressed, oppressed, then we will suffer a sickness of the soul. The gap between what the culture asks of us and what the gods wish of us will be labeled with a scientific sounding word, *neurosis*, but it is not a disorder of the nervous system. It is a split that one sees in the archaic picture of Eden, the split between eating of the tree of life and the tree of knowledge, of suffering conflict between the agenda of instinct and the agenda of mind. Oppressing the animating energy of the gods will be called depression. Hungering for transcendent engagement will eventuate as eating disorders, addictions, obsessions and paraphilias.

The suffering of the soul which is unmet will manifest as sociopathy, narcissistic disorder, schizoid splitting and deep, deep loneliness. Gods who are not acknowledged will breed monsters. An institution which seeks control over the powers of nature will sooner or later have to pay its dues to nature, as the scandals of clerical abuse of their flock so sadly demonstrate. Their psychotherapeutic colleagues, armed with strong ethical and legal statements, are perhaps no better; some studies have indicated that as many as ten per cent have acted out inappropriately with their clients.

The gods of our nature will not be mocked; they will have their due recognition or will take revenge as psychosomatic disorder, as depression, or as unconscious enactment. Again, we recall that a deity is the personification of spiritual energy. To forget that energy which lies behind the image is to function unconsciously. From this flaw in our nature is forged the stuff of tragedy.

Reorganized innocence

William Blake's summons to "reorganized innocence" is at best an oxymoron, at worst impossible. What could he mean? How could one ever regain the prelapsarian state, be as open, see the world as appareled in luminosity, as those first souls, themselves metaphors, Adam and Eve, whose etymological roots intimate *earth* and *animation* respectively?

Even as "animated matter" we have grown dulled to the enspirited world. Reiteration, the weight of daily drudge, the invisible silica of the mundane, weighs heavily upon us. We need to recover access to the gods, surely, and it will not come from thumping on the tub of history by seeking to force *pneuma* back into the old husks. Remember, the gods have not gone; they have left the old husks, but are alive and well elsewhere. So the problem becomes our capacity to see them.

We recall the reported words of Jesus in the Gnostic Gospel of Thomas that the kingdom of God is spread all over this world and we do not see it. The surrealist poet Paul Eluard famously observed, "There is another world, and this is it."

The problem is our seeing again, or anew. This is why Freud and Jung became necessary, why depth psychology is critical to the formation of the postmodern sensibility, and why each of us has to return to the smithy of the private soul to find the new images which the gods send us, as they surely will, as surely as we will dream tonight, with or without ego attentiveness.

In Joseph Campbell's phrase, we are challenged to become "transparent to transcendence."[102] What does this mean to each of us? The natural tendency of our conscious lives inclines toward objectifying reality and seeking to master it, to serve the anxiety management agenda of the ego. Most modern psychology is an example of this tendency and therefore focuses upon

---

[102] *Thou Art That: Transforming Religious Metaphor*, p. 18.

behavior rather than meaning, management rather than therapy and all in service to the subordination of the gods to that great demanding super-god: Security.

When we succumb to this agenda, we are inclined to the reification of images, the fantasy of their mastery, or at least their manipulation, and accordingly the energy does not shine through them. We are, in short, in contact with the husk and not the divine *pneuma,* the spirit which blows through the husk to render it numinous. The sheer wonder of dreams, the incredible creative process of their imagery, their strange scenarios, their startling agendas, is itself a visitation by divine energy. Those who are "institutionalized" will deny that such manifestation is divine, fearing that it may summon them to agendas which call for crucifixion, transformation, death. And they are probably right in this premonition. But still, when we, as conscious beings, are in the presence of such autonomous, transcendent energy, we are in the presence of the gods.

I have often suggested that people sit back and ask themselves from whence their dream has come. Did they invent it? Did I invent it for them? Does it come from the Self, whatever that is? To abide awhile in the mystery of the manifest gift of the dream is to recover awe, and the possibility of a right relationship to the divine. In other words, one is "transparent to transcendence." The sacred energy flows through an image to us, through us, rather than we fixating upon the image, worshipping Jesus or the Buddha or some other charismatic figure.

The influence of these figures upon their contemporaries must have been so compelling because they were diaphanous, that is, light showed through them, energy suffused them and touched something deep within those around them. This, too, is surely what-Blake meant when he said he saw eternity in a grain of sand, and that the doors of perception, once cleansed, behold eternity:

To see a World in a Grain of Sand
And a Heaven in a Wild Flower
Hold Infinity in the palm of your hand
And eternity in an hour.... [103]

Jung thought on these matters and offered deep insights. While Blake could still speak of the force that so animated the grain of sand that he could see through to Zion's shores, we are less likely to have the affective linkage to the old images that obtained for Blake. Jung says that we can still approach the holy precincts, if not by way of Zion, at least by way of the psyche, which is the arena in which all our meaning events occur. He writes:

> I strip things of their metaphysical wrapping in order to make them objects of psychology. In that way I can . . . discover psychological facts and processes that before were veiled in symbols beyond my comprehension. In doing so I may perhaps be following in the steps of the faithful, and may possibly have similar experiences; and if to the end there should be something ineffably metaphysical behind it all, it would have the best opportunity of showing itself.[104]

This is the sort of statement by Jung that infuriates some folks. They claim he is "psychologizing" God, as if God were a mere epiphenomenon of the psyche. Whatever the gods are, they are inevitably experienced intrapsychically, as all our experiences occur, whether they derive from outer or inner causation. What Jung is seeking to preserve here is the validity of and accessibility to the meaning of a god-event. Whether occasioned by an outer metaphysical being, or as an intrapsychic manifestation, the event is real for us, and worthy of our respect.

As Jung says, this attitude allows for what is most important, the experience of incarnated meaning, rather than privileging

---

[103] "Auguries of Innocence," in *The Poetry and Prose of William Blake*, p. 481.
[104] "Secret of the Golden Flower," *Alchemical Studies*, CW 13, par. 73.

the ego's anxiety to fixate a cause and thereby rest easy in Zion. With this openness, Jung argues, whatever metaphysical realities there are may more abundantly manifest. Either way, one becomes transparent to the transcendent. As we all know, the early history of the Bible reports divinity repeatedly chastising the faithful for reifying their divine experience, transforming the spirit into images. We are not superior to our predecessors; we are all prone to idolatry when we forget that the image is meant to point beyond itself toward the ineffable. The symbol points toward the godly, but it is not the god.

As noted earlier, this idolatrous confusion leads to literalism, pogroms and crusades. It is bad psychology and bad theology.

In the end, both psychologist and theologian must respect the ineffable. Psychology no more knows what the psyche is than the theologian knows what God is. Anyone who thinks otherwise, and proclaims otherwise, is deluded, inflated or psychotic. "God" is a metaphor for what wholly transcends our capacity to comprehend, expressed through primal forces which we nonetheless experience. (To use the word *God* is a form of respect for that suprapersonal energy.) The word *psyche* is a metaphor for what wholly transcends our capacity to comprehend, forces at work within each of us. (The use of that word *psyche* is possible only if we retain our respect for the ineffable, lest we deteriorate into the fantasy of psychology, which is the fantasy of controlling that which lies beyond our powers.)

For both psychology and theology, the proper religious attitudes are awe and humility before the unknown. Anything else is self-delusion. As Jung writes of the arcana of the medieval shamanic healers,

> We should not begrudge Paracelsus and the alchemists their secret language. . . . The protean mythologem and the shimmering symbol express the processes of the psyche far more trenchantly and, in the end, far more clearly than the clearest concept; for the symbol not

only conveys a visualization of the process but . . . it also brings a re-experiencing of it.[105]

Speaking of alchemy, what are we to make of a dream brought to me last week by a fifty-some-year-old woman, a person who has not studied alchemy at all? These are her notes:

A clear liquid is brewing in a pot over a hotplate in a lab. I drop balls of mercury (like from a thermometer, quicksilver) into the pot. With a tool, I roll it around—several of the drops of mercury turn into nuggets of gold. It seems that they were to be put into something else; however, I am fascinated with what I see happening. I pick up one of the nuggets to feel it and it goes up in a puff of smoke!

There is a sign over the lab table that says, "Do not pick up, the gas is poisonous!"

In fascination and disbelief, I do it again. I go to tell a lab technician about what I have done and ask what I should do. He is standing behind a counter like a dispensing pharmacist. He hands me two kinds of salts and tells me to take a certain amount. I say that I do not have a way to measure the salts. In disgust, they measure it out and put it in my mouth.

In the objective, outer world, she had recently been given a special diet of salts to regulate blood pressure. And she had just completed an unusually successful visit to her mother who had typically sought control of her life. This time the dreamer indicated she had been able to listen to her mother, not be complexed by her provocative probes, and knew "if I needed to leave, I could have. I was a free agent. I didn't give myself up and I just let the hours roll forward one after the other."

While this dream could lend itself to endless amplification, it is important to notice that the central task of this woman, as is true for all people over forty, is to find her own truth, her own

---

[105] "Paracelsus as a Spiritual Phenomenon," ibid., par. 199.

authority, and to risk living it. In alchemical literature, mercury is associated with the transformative attributes of Hermes, agent of change and hidden moves. She had felt that she had to be somewhat hermetic in her meeting with her mother: reveal, yes, but more often conceal.

Her whole analytic process has addressed the task of transformation, to which she herself has brought many substantive contributions. Yet, at the very moment the silver is transformed into gold, she believed she was overeager to grasp the change, fix the development, so it explodes on her, with possible toxic effects. (Near the same time she dreamt of a child without hands, which, as we know from the fairy tale "The Handless Maiden," suggests a severing of will from agency, hands being instruments of action).

In the midst of this struggle for authority and freedom, she is seemingly cautioned by her own psyche about presuming to grab the gold too soon. More process is required. The salt which she must learn to take patiently is a catalytic agent. Just as she had to be careful to moderate her salt intake, so she is obliged to undertake this change in a measured manner as well. The gold is surely there, but the toxic mercury vapor is also there. This *opus* will take time. Consciousness must wait upon psyche's rhythms.

Again we must ask, from where do these images come? The dreamer was not familiar with alchemical literature though she distantly knew Jung was interested in it. Such arcane images, such magic, reveal the movement of mysteries within the psyche. Any analyst can recall dozens of remarkable dreams from analysands over the years: some presenting stunning perspectives on real life problems; others of seeming banal origin; others again coming from no conscious frame of reference but bearing the imprint of mysteries nonetheless.

These images come from the imaginal world which lies between the world of our physical perceptions and the realm of the gods. The meeting point, perhaps occasioned by the activity of the Self which Jung called "the transcendent function," is an autonomous activity of the psyche which seeks to bridge the gap between conscious and unconscious realms. Attending this meeting point is the chief office of depth therapy, as well as the mystical traditions found in all the great religions and in the private souls of individuals. This is the realm where creative enterprise is found, where revelation is offered, where one is enlarged. The image which arises, we recall, is not the god; rather, the god has suffused the image with numinosity. But it is through the image that we may both approach and receive the gods.

Active imagination

Jung's technique of active imagination is rather well known, yet to this day it remains confused with meditation, directive imaging and free association. But, as the name suggests, in active imagination consciousness respectfully approaches the image, activates it through engagement, and then pays attention to what the image wishes to do. To the insecure, such an open-ended exercise threatens to undermine the ego's platform. There are many practicing psychologists who do not believe the unconscious exists, or that they need take dialogue with it seriously, even though the unconscious denied is thereby granted even more autonomy. For all their education, they do not know enough to know that they do not know enough.

It is like the timid using exhausted dogmas or reiterated ritual as an apotropaic defense against religious experience. What if the gods actually spoke to them? They would then have to live with a larger burden of responsibility.

Active imagination is the work of a strong and willing ego, an ego open to insight, development, revelation. The skeptical ego will say, "Oh, but I am just making this up." And at times, the ego clearly does interfere. But generally one finds a life within the image which presents perhaps a puzzling figure from a dream, perhaps a motif in one's history. The ego's task is to hold its own, watch, interact, and record the unfolding in some fashion such as writing, image making, or movement. These images come to us from the mystery which is invested not only in the cosmos, but in each of us.

Jung provides a good example of this process in his memoir, *Memories, Dreams, Reflections,* whereby he developed an active relationship with the images which came to him from the unconscious. It is no accident that he chose those three words to title his book. Memory helps us discern not only pattern, but the invisible hand which plays a role in creating the pattern. And dreams come from a place outside the control of consciousness. Yet, by seriously reflecting on both pattern and dream, the individual takes responsibility for change, for acknowledgement, for ethical choice.

Such a personal, direct access to the mysteries renders us less passive in the presence of the gods. We invite them, though invited or not they will be present. Uninvited, they will come to us as pathologies. It is not true that the gods have disappeared. The teleological energies they embody are omnipresent, speaking, and revealing that the manifest world and the invisible world are one. To repeat Marcus Aurelius once more on the gods, "It is experience which proves their power every day, and therefore I am satisfied that they exist, and I do them reverence."[106]

The faithful will protest that we make the gods "a mere myth," a "psychologism," a "disrespectful fiction." But as long as the gods are thought of as facts rather than as metaphors, or symbols which point beyond themselves to the mystery, then they will be hoist on the petard of observable empiricism, and we entirely miss the possibility of spiritual transformation.

---

[106] *Meditations,* p. 186.

For those who reject this view, daily life is uninformed by depth or mystery. But life without depth or mystery is brutally sterile. Recall Pozzo and Lucky in *Waiting for Godot:* there is nowhere to go, nothing to do, because there is no hierarchical plane, only the horizontal upon which they sit and wait. But to call the movement of the psyche, the rhythms of heart and surge of blood, and the unfolding motifs of history the work of the gods is to honor them, to recover depth and perspective.

The nineteenth-century poet Stephan Mallarmé, wrestling with this twin dilemma, wrote,

> Yes, *I know*, we are nothing but vain forms of matter—yet sublime too when you think that we invented God and our own souls. So sublime . . . that I want to give this spectacle of a matter aware, yes, of what it is but throwing itself madly into the Dream that it knows it is not, singing the Soul and all those divine impressions that gather in us from earliest childhood, and proclaiming before the Nothingness that is the truth, those glorious falsehoods.[107]

Mallarmé is not afraid of the tension of opposites, and his argument is a tad more subtle than first read. We are vain forms of matter, yet possessing some faculty capable of imagining the gods, that is, of evolving the metaphors which point to the mysterious plane we tread. We are "matter aware"—matter capable of reflection, capable of metaphor and symbol as no other form of life seems to be. We are the symbol-making animal, and, therefore, the animal who lives not just by instinct but by meaning. We are the animal that can not only experience grief, pride, joy, fear, and many more psychic states, but reflect upon them as well.

The psyche reflecting upon itself is a manifestation of the spirit, that which differentiates us from the simple slug or leviathan. Part of our instinctual reality seeks to make metaphors,

---

[107] Cited by Calasso, *Literature and the Gods,* p. 111.

and that is how our radical amazement at life takes phenomenological form. Concept, structure, classification, even institutionalized ossification, come later. "Knowing," "experiencing"
and "meaning" are concurrent and rendered into consciousness
by metaphor. So we do the gods honor when we live our lives
one mythologem at a time, populate the myth of our journey,
and the myth of our time, with their divine presences acknowledged as co-participant.

We no longer live in an animistic age where the gods are visible in the flight of birds, in the ever-branching trees, in the spi-
raling smoke of a camp fire. We have fallen into a world of objects from which the gods seem banished. Though we have gained
enormous power to move those objects to our will, yet we live
more superficially and frantically than ever. Only an appreciation of metaphor can render the invisible world visible again.
The gods are there whenever the ego and the Self meet, when an
image emerges from this congruence, and when consciousness
can open to the wonder which all this brings.

Reflecting on a dream, Jung writes,

> Through this dream I understood that the self is the principle and
> the archetype of orientation and meaning. Therein lies its healing
> function. For me, this insight signified an approach to the center
> and therefore to the goal. Out of it emerged a first inkling of my
> personal myth.[108]

Thus, our relationship to the infinite powers which move not
only the sidereal bodies but course through our own mortally
fleeting frames as well, is opened by the engagement with metaphor, the knowing wink of the eye which reveals that we are not
bewitched by our own mental constructs into reifying the gods.
We use our fictions consciously and therefore are not enslaved
to them. Instead, they enable us to move into proximity with

---

[108] *Memories,* p. 199.

the invisible world. As Rilke's fictional persona, Malte Laurids Brigge, put it,

> I am learning to see. I don't know why it is, but everything pene-trates more deeply into me and does not stop at the place where un-til now it always used to finish. I have an inner self of which I was ignorant. Every thing goes thither now. What happens there I do not know.[109]

Each of us needs to recall what our ancestors knew: that there is an autonomous place within us which, if we trust it and dia-logue in a disciplined way, will speak to us and offer us guidance.

As scientist, physician, shaman, therapist and scholar, Jung was able to open himself to mystery. He did not invent, but cer-tainly helped recover, a way for the modern to appreciate the spiritual. He exclaims, "My works are a more or less successful endeavor to incorporate this incandescent matter into the con-temporary picture of the world."[110]

And lastly from Jung, we need to be reminded,

> The need for mythic statements is satisfied when we frame a view of the world which adequately explains the meaning of human exis-tence in the cosmos, a view which springs from our psychic whole-ness, from the co-operation between conscious and unconscious. Meaninglessness inhibits fullness of life and is therefore equivalent to illness. Meaning makes a great many things endurable—perhaps everything. No science will ever replace myth, and a myth cannot be made out of any science. For it is not that "God" is a myth, but that myth is the revelation of a divine life in man.[111]

The makers of myth in our time are you and I—in the dreams we dream, in the patterns we weave, and in those unpredictable momentary apertures into eternity through which we catch a

---

[109] *The Notebook of Malte Laurids Brigge*, pp. 14f.
[110] *Memories*, p. 199.
[111] Ibid., p. 340.

glimpse of the passing forms of gods. Our material world floats on a sea of anxiety, yet is resolutely sustained by invisible threads. Nowhere is this more true than when one believes the gods are wholly gone.

As orphic voyagers who return to the visible world bearing metaphors, the poets have much to tell us about these matters. In a poem titled "The Death of God," Stephen Dunn notes this paradox—the invisible gods, just below the surface of visible things:

> God took his invisible place in the kingdom of need.
> Disaffected minstrels made and sang His songs.
> The angels were given breath and brain.
> This all went on while He was dead in the world.[112]

Even in a time of dearth, the disbelieving poet intuits the movement of divinities in the invisible realm:

> . . . hundreds of stars flicking *if, if, if.*
> Everywhere in the universe, it seemed,
> some next thing was gathering itself.[113]

All the while we fantasize that we are building our kingdoms of volitional intent, death is

> tampering with airbrakes,
> scattering cancer cells like seed,
> loosening the wooden beams of roller coasters.[114]

And history, seemingly past, invisibly informs each moment when we presume we really know enough to make the right and different choices. And all the while, the dead,

> are looking down through the glass-bottom boats of heaven

---

[112] *Different Hours,* p. 27.
[113] Dunn, "Zero Hour," in ibid., p. 43.
[114] "My Number," in Billy Collins, *Sailing Alone Around the Room*, p. 15.

as they row themselves slowly through eternity. [115]

The gods are present whenever we ask the right questions about our journeys. Knowing what questions matter is the first and nearly most difficult task. Living the answers the gods bring to us, in lieu of those we would prefer, is the greater challenge. As Carl Dennis asks,

> Am I leading the life that my soul,
> Mortal or not, wants me to lead is a question
> That seems at least as meaningful as the question
> Am I leading the life I want to live . . . .[116]

In the great round of the stars, and in the flurry and flush of our fevered days, some force moves us through all things toward ends unknown. We honor that invisible force through this metaphor: *the gods*.

> Not till you reach the watery crossing
> Will he leave your side, and even then
> He'll shout instructions as you slip from your shoes
> And wade alone into that dark river.[117]

---

[115] "The Dead," in ibid., p. 33.
[116] "A Chance for the Soul," in Dennis, *Practical Gods*, p. 30.
[117] "A Priest of Hermes," in ibid., p. 1.

Bibliography

Agee, James. *A Death in the Family*. New York: Bantam, 1957.

Aurelius, Marcus. *Meditations*. Trans. Maxwell Staniforth. London: Penguin, 1964.

Barfield, Owen. *Saving the Appearances: A Study in Idolatry*. London: Faber and Faber, 1957.

Barth, John. "The Night-Sea Journey." In *Lost in the Funhouse*. New York: Doubleday, 1968.

Beckett, Samuel. *Waiting for Godot*. New York: Grove Press, 1997.

Blake, William. *The Poetry and Prose of William Blake*. Ed. David K. Erdman. Garden City, NY: Doubleday, 1965.

Bly, Robert, Hillman, James, Meade Michael, eds. *The Rag and Bone Shop of the Heart: Poems for Men*. New York: HarperCollins, 1992.

Bonhoeffer, Dietrich. *Letters and Papers from Prison*. Trans. Eberhard Bethge. New York: Macmillan, 1953.

Brecht, Bertholt. *Galileo*. New York: Grove Press, 1991.

Burlingame, Michael. *The Inner World of Abraham Lincoln*. Urbana, IL: University of Illinois Press, 1994.

Calasso, Roberto. *Literature and the Gods*. New York: Alfred A. Knopf. 2001.

Campbell, Joseph. *The Hero with a Thousand Faces* (Bollingen Series XVII). Princeton: Princeton University Press, 1972

_____. *Thou Art That: Transforming Religious Metaphor*. Novato, CA: New World Library, 2001.

Camus, Albert. *The Stranger*. New York: Knopf, 1988.

Collins, Billy. *Sailing Alone Around the Room*. New York: Random House, 2001.

Dahl, Roald. *Kiss, Kiss*. New York: Random House, 1959.

Dennis, Carl. *Practical Gods*. New York: Penguin, 2001.

Diagnostic Criteria from DSM-IV. Washington, DC: American Psychiatric Association, 1994.

Donaghue, Denis, ed. *The Complete Poetry and Selected Prose of John Donne.* New York: Modern Library, 2001.

Downing, Christine. *Gods in Our Midst: Mythological Images of the Masculine: A Woman's View.* New York: Crossroad Publishing, 1993.

Dunn, Stephen. *Different Hours.* New York: W.W. Norton and Co., 2000.

Eliot, T.S. *The Complete Poems and Plays: 1909-1950.* New York: Harcourt, Brace, and World. 1962.

Flaubert, Gustave. "A Simple Heart." In *Three Tales.* New York: Penguin, 1961.

Heidegger, Martin. *Being and Time.* San Francisco, CA: HarperCollins, 1962.

Henderson, Joseph L. *Cultural Attitudes in Psychological Perspective.* Toronto: Inner City Books, 1984.

Hoeller, Stephan A. *The Gnostic Jung and the Seven Sermons to the Dead.* Wheaton, IL: Theosophical Publishing House, 1982.

Hollis, James. *On This Journey We Call Our Life: Living the Questions.* Toronto: Inner City Books, 2003.

_____. *Tracking the Gods: The Place of Myth in Everyday Life.* Toronto: Inner City Books, 1995.

Homer. *War Music.* Trans. Christopher Logue. New York: Faber and Faber, Inc., 2001.

Jung, C.G. *The Collected Works.* (Bollingen Series XX) 20 vols. Trans. R.F.C. Hull. Ed. H. Read, M. Fordham, G. Adler, Wm. McGuire. Princeton: Princeton University Press, 1953-79.

_____. *Man and His Symbols.* New York: Doubleday and Co., 1964.

_____. *Memories, Dreams, Reflections.* Ed. Aniela Jaffé. New York: Pantheon Books, 1961.

Kafka, Franz. *Selected Short Stories*. Trans. Willa and Edwin Muir. New York: The Modern Library, 1952.

Kierkegaard, Soren. *Concluding Unscientific Postscript*. Ed. Howard Hong and Edna Hong. Princeton: Princeton University Press, 1992.

Kripal, Jeffrey J. *Kali's Child: the Mystical and Erotic in the Life and Teachings of Ramakrishna*. Chicago: University of Chicago Press, 1995.

Kundera, Milan. *Identity*. New York: HarperFlamingo, 1998.

Koeppen, Wolfgang. *Death in Rome*. Trans. Michael Hofmann. New York: W.W. Norton & Co., 1954.

Matthews, William. "The Psychopathology of Everyday Life." In *The Norton Introduction to Poetry*. Ed. J. Paul Hunter. New York: Norton and Norton, 1973.

McGuire, William, and Hull, R.F.C., eds. *C.G. Jung Speaking*. Princeton: Princeton University Press, 1977.

Musil, Robert. *The Man Without Qualities*. New York: Perigee Books, 1980.

Nasar, Sylvia. *A Beautiful Mind: The Life of Mathematical Genius and Nobel Laureate John Nash*. New York: Simon and Schuster, 1998..

Nietzsche, Friedrich. *The Portable Nietzsche*. Ed. Walter Kaufmann. New York: Viking, 1972.

The Norton Anthology of Poetry. 3rd edition. Ed. Alexander Alison et al. New York: W.W. Norton and Company, 1983.

Ovid. *Metamorphoses*. Trans. Mary M. Innes. London: Penguin Books, 1995.

Oz, Amos. *The Same Sea*. Trans. Nicholas de Lange. New York: Harcourt, Inc. 1999.

Paris, Ginette. *Pagan Grace: Dionysos, Hermes and Goddess Memory* in *Daily Life*. Woodstock, CT: Spring Publications, 1990.

_____. *Pagan Meditations: The Worlds of Aphrodite, Artemis, and Hestia*. Woodstock, CT: Spring Publications, 1986.

Perse, Saint-John. *Anabasis.* Trans. T.S. Eliot. New York: Harcourt, Brace, Jovanovich, 1949.

Plath, Sylvia. *The Collected Poems.* New York: Harper and Row, 1981.

Rilke, Rainer Maria. *The Duino Elegies.* Trans. J.B. Leishman and Stephen Spender. New York: Norton, 1967.

_____. *The Notebook of Malte Laurids Brigge.* Trans. M.D. Herter Norton. New York: W.W. Norton and Co., 1949.

_____. *Sonnets to Orpheus.* New York: W.W. Norton Inc., 1962.

Rosenthal, M.L., ed. *Selected Poems and Two Plays of William Butler Yeats.* New York: Macmillan, 1962.

Schopenhauer, Arthur. *Samtliche Werke.* Frankfurt: Verlag der Corraschen Buchhandlung, 1895-98.

Sharp, Daryl. *The Secret Raven: Conflict and Transformation in the Life of Franz Kafka.* Toronto: Inner City Books, 1980.

Slochower, Harry. *Mythopoesis: Mythic Patterns in the Literary Classics.* Detroit: Wayne State University Press, 1970.

Stern, Paul. *C.G. Jung: The Haunted Prophet.* New York: George Braziller, 1976.

Tarnas, Richard. *Prometheus the Awakener.* Woodstock, CT: Spring Publications, 1995.

Thomas, Dylan. *Collected Poems.* New York: New Directions Publishing Co., 1946.

Tillich, Paul. *The Courage To Be.* Newhaven, CT: Yale University Press, 1980.

Waley, Arthur. *The Way and Its Power.* New York: Grove Press, 1958.

Wordsworth, William. *William Wordsworth: The Major Works.* Oxford, UK: Oxford University Press, 2000.

Yeats, W.B., ed. *The Oxford Book of Modern Verse.* Oxford, UK: Oxford University Press, 1936.

Index

Also by James Hollis in this Series

THE MIDDLE PASSAGE: From Misery to Meaning in Midlife
ISBN 0-919123-60-0. (1993) 128pp. *Sewn* $16
Why do so many go through so much disruption in their middle years? What does it mean and how can we survive it? Hollis shows how we can pass through midlife consciously, rendering the second half of life all the richer and more meaningful.

UNDER SATURN'S SHADOW: The Wounding and Healing of Men
ISBN 0-919123-64-3. (1994) 144pp. *Sewn* $18
Saturn was the Roman god who ate his children to stop them from usurping his power. Men have been psychologically and spiritually wounded by this legacy. Hollis offers a new perspective on the secrets men carry in their hearts, and how they may be healed.

TRACKING THE GODS: The Place of Myth in Modern Life
ISBN 0-919123-69-4. (1995) 160pp. *Sewn* $18
Whatever our religious background or personal psychology, a greater intimacy with myth provides a vital link with meaning. Here Hollis explains why a connection with our mythic roots is crucial for us as individuals and as responsible citizens.

SWAMPLANDS OF THE SOUL: New Life in Dismal Places
ISBN 0-919123-74-0. (1996) 160pp. *Sewn* $18
Much of our time on earth we are lost in the quicksands of guilt, anxiety, betrayal, grief, doubt, loss, loneliness, despair, anger, obsessions, addictions, depression and the like. Perhaps the goal of life is not happiness but meaning. Hollis illuminates the way.

THE EDEN PROJECT: In Search of the Magical Other
ISBN 0-919123-80-5. (1998) 160pp. *Sewn* $18
A timely and thought-provoking corrective to the fantasies about relationships that permeate Western culture. Here is a challenge to greater personal responsibility—a call for individual growth as opposed to seeking rescue from others.

CREATING A LIFE: Finding Your Individual Path
ISBN 0-919123-93-7. (2001) 160pp. *Sewn* $18
With insight and compassion grounded in the humanist side of analytical psychology, Hollis elucidates the circuitous path of individuation, illustrating how we may come to understand our life choices and relationships by exploring our core complexes.

ON THIS JOURNEY WE CALL OUR LIFE: Living the Questions
ISBN 1-894574-04-4. (2003) 160pp. *Sewn* $18
This book seeks a working partnership with readers. Hollis shares his personal experience only so that we may more deeply understand our own. It is a partnership rich in poetry as well as prose, but most of all it reminds us of the treasures of uncertainty.

Studies in Jungian Psychology
by Jungian Analysts

Quality Paperbacks

Prices and payment in $US (except in Canada, $Cdn)

Alchemy: An Introduction to the Symbolism and the Psychology
Marie-Louise von Franz (Zurich) ISBN 0-919123-04-X. 288 pp. $22

Jung and Yoga: The Psyche-Body Connection
Judith Harris (London, Ontario) ISBN 0-919123-95-3. 160 pp. $18

Jungian Psychology Unplugged: My Life as an Elephant
Daryl Sharp (Toronto) ISBN 0-919123-81-3. 160 pp. $18

Conscious Femininity: Interviews with Marion Woodman
Introduction by Marion Woodman (Toronto) ISBN 0-919123-59-7. 160 pp. $18

The Sacred Psyche: A Psychological Approach to the Psalms
Edward F. Edinger (Los Angeles) ISBN 1-894574-09-5. 160 pp. $18

Eros and Pathos: Shades of Love and Suffering
Aldo Carotenuto (Rome) ISBN 0-919123-39-2. 144 pp. $18

Descent to the Goddess: A Way of Initiation for Women
Sylvia Brinton Perera (New York) ISBN 0-919123-05-8. 112 pp. $16

Addiction to Perfection: The Still Unravished Bride
Marion Woodman (Toronto) ISBN 0-919123-11-2. Illustrated. 208 pp. $20pb/$25hc

The Illness That We Are: A Jungian Critique of Christianity
John P. Dourley (Ottawa) ISBN 0-919123-16-3. 128 pp. $16

Coming To Age: The Croning Years and Late-Life Transformation
Jane R. Prétat (Providence) ISBN 0-919123-63-5. 144 pp. $18

Jungian Dream Interpretation: A Handbook of Theory and Practice
James A. Hall, M.D. (Dallas) ISBN 0-919123-12-0. 128 pp. $16

Phallos: Sacred Image of the Masculine
Eugene Monick (Scranton) ISBN 0-919123-26-0. 30 illustrations. 144 pp. $18

The Sacred Prostitute: Eternal Aspect of the Feminine
Nancy Qualls-Corbett (Birmingham) ISBN 0-919123-31-7. 20 illustrations. 176 pp. $20

Personality Types: Jung's Model of Typology
Daryl Sharp (Toronto) ISBN 0-919123-30-9. 128 pp. $16

The Pregnant Virgin: A Process of Psychological Development
Marion Woodman (Toronto) ISBN 0-919123-20-1. 28 illustrations. 208 pp. $20pb/$25hc

Discounts: any 3-5 books, 10%; 6-9 books, 20%; 10 or more, 25%
Add Postage/Handling: 1-2 books, $6 surface ($10 air); 3-4 books, $8 surface ($12 air);
*   5-9 books, $15 surface ($20 air); 10 or more, $10 surface ($25 air)*

Ask for **Jung at Heart** newsletter and free Catalogue of **over 100 titles**

INNER CITY BOOKS
Box 1271, Station Q, Toronto, ON M4T 2P4, Canada

Tel. (416) 927-0355 / Fax (416) 924-1814 / E-mail: sales@innercitybooks.net